Jennifer Hudson

Other books in the People in the News series:

Maya Angelou

Tyra Banks

David Beckham

Beyoncé

Sandra Bullock

Fidel Castro

Kelly Clarkson

Hillary Clinton

Miley Cyrus

Ellen Degeneres

Leonardo DiCaprio

Hilary Duff

Zac Efron

Brett Favre

50 Cent

Al Gore

Tony Hawk

Salma Hayek

LeBron James

Jay-Z

Derek Jeter

Steve Jobs

Dwayne Johnson

Angelina Jolie

Jonas Brothers

Kim Jong II

Hamid Karzai

Coretta Scott King

Ashton Kutcher

Lady Gaga

George Lopez

Bernie Madoff

Tobey Maguire

Eli Manning

John McCain

Barack Obama

Michelle Obama

Danica Patrick

Nancy Pelosi

Tyler Perry

Michael Phelps

Queen Latifah

Daniel Radcliffe

Condoleezza Rice

Rihanna

Alex Rodriguez

J.K. Rowling

Shakira

Tupac Shakur

Will Smith

Sonia Sotomayor

Gwen Stefani

Ben Stiller

Hilary Swank

Justin Timberlake

Usher

Denzel Washington

Serena Williams

Oprah Winfrey

Jennifer Hudson

by Cherese Cartlidge

LUCENT BOOKS

A part of Gale, Cengage Learning

GALE
CENGAGE Learning

Detroit • New York • San Francisco • New Haven, Conn • Waterville, Maine • London

LIBRARY OF CONGRESS CATALOGING-IN-PUBLICATION DATA

Cartlidge, Cherese.
Jennifer Hudson / by Cherese Cartlidge.
   p. cm. -- (People in the news)
Includes bibliographical references and index.
ISBN 978-1-4205-0607-5 (hardcover)
1. Hudson, Jennifer, 1981---Juvenile literature. 2. Singers--United States--Biography--Juvenile literature. 3. Motion picture actors and actresses--United States--Biography--Juvenile literature. I. Title.
ML3930.H82C37 2011
782.42164092--dc22
[B]

2011006366

Lucent Books
27500 Drake Rd
Farmington Hills MI 48331

ISBN-13: 978-1-4205-0607-5
ISBN-10: 1-4205-0607-2

Printed in the United States of America
1 2 3 4 5 6 7 15 14 13 12 11

Printed by Bang Printing, Brainerd, MN, 1st Ptg., 06/2011

Contents

Fame and celebrity are alluring. People are drawn to those who walk in fame's spotlight, whether they are known for great accomplishments or for notorious deeds. The lives of the famous pique public interest and attract attention, perhaps because their experiences seem in some ways so different from, yet in other ways so similar to, our own.

Newspapers, magazines, and television regularly capitalize on this fascination with celebrity by running profiles of famous people. For example, television programs such as *Entertainment Tonight* devote all their programming to stories about entertainment and entertainers. Magazines such as *People* fill their pages with stories of the private lives of famous people. Even newspapers, newsmagazines, and television news frequently delve into the lives of well-known personalities. Despite the number of articles and programs, few provide more than a superficial glimpse at their subjects.

Lucent's People in the News series offers young readers a deeper look into the lives of today's newsmakers, the influences that have shaped them, and the impact they have had in their fields of endeavor and on other people's lives. The subjects of the series hail from many disciplines and walks of life. They include authors, musicians, athletes, political leaders, entertainers, entrepreneurs, and others who have made a mark on modern life and who, in many cases, will continue to do so for years to come.

These biographies are more than factual chronicles. Each book emphasizes the contributions, accomplishments, or deeds that have brought fame or notoriety to the individual and shows how that person has influenced modern life. Authors portray their subjects in a realistic, unsentimental light. For example, Bill Gates – the cofounder and chief executive officer of the software giant Microsoft – has been instrumental in making personal computers the most vital tool of the modern age. Few dispute his business savvy, his perseverance, or his technical expertise, yet critics say he is ruthless in his dealings with competitors and driven more by his desire to maintain Microsoft's dominance in the computer industry than by an interest in furthering technology.

In these books, young readers will encounter inspiring stories about real people who achieved success despite enormous obstacles. Oprah Winfrey – the most powerful, most watched, and wealthiest woman on television today – spent the first six years of her life in the care of her grandparents while her unwed mother sought work and a better life elsewhere. Her adolescence was colored by rape, pregnancy at age fourteen, and sexual abuse.

Each author documents and supports his or her work with an array of primary and secondary source quotations taken from diaries, letters, speeches, and interviews. All quotes are footnoted to show readers exactly how and where biographers derive their information and provide guidance for further research. The quotations enliven the text by giving readers eyewitness views of the life and accomplishments of each person covered in the People in the News series.

In addition, each book in the series includes photographs, annotated bibliographies, timelines, and comprehensive indexes. For both the casual reader and the student researcher, the People in the News series offers insight into the lives of today's newsmakers – people who shape the way we live, work, and play in the modern age.

A Chicago Girl

Jennifer Hudson is proud of her hometown. Born and raised on the South Side of Chicago, Illinois, Hudson has not forgotten her roots there, even after her tremendous success as a singer and actress. "Home is Chicago,"[1] she told talk show host David Letterman after the release of her first film, *Dreamgirls* (2006). Indeed, the first house she purchased, bought the same year *Dreamgirls* hit theaters, is in Chicago.

The success and triumphs the Oscar-winning Hudson has achieved have not come easily. Her appearance in 2004 as a contestant on the third season of *American Idol* was filled with challenges, not the least of which was being voted off in the semifinals. Though she was brought back to the show as one of eight wild card contestants, she wound up being voted off a second time. There were personal challenges in her life as well, including the loss of her beloved grandmother in 1998, followed a year later by the death of her stepfather. Then an unimaginable personal tragedy occurred in 2008: three close family members were brutally murdered. It took Hudson several months to come to grips with the shock and grief she felt over their deaths, during which time she retreated from public appearances. She returned to performing in early 2009 with a whirlwind of triumphant appearances. In her personal life, as well, she has rebounded from the family tragedy, with a new son and a fiancé now at the center of her life.

The city Hudson calls home has faced its share of triumphs

and challenges, just as she has. Chicago was founded in 1833 on the southwestern shore of Lake Michigan with a population of roughly two hundred people. In the mid-1800s, Chicago emerged as a center of industry and a major transportation hub. Disaster struck the city in 1871: The Great Chicago Fire, which raged for two days and claimed hundreds of lives, took with it a third of the city. About 4 square miles (10 sq. km) of the city was destroyed, leaving the business district a burned-out shell and approximately ninety thousand people homeless. Just as Hudson has rebounded from tragedy, so too did her fellow Chicagoans. After the fire, the city experienced rapid rebuilding and growth, and in 1885 the world's first skyscraper was erected in downtown Chicago. Today Chicago is the nation's third most populated city, with more than 2.8 million residents, and is home to O'Hare International Airport, the second-busiest airport in the world.

"I Have to Stand in Line Like Everybody Else"

Jennifer Hudson grew up in a white, two-story house in the 7000 block of South Yale Avenue in Chicago. Some of her neighbors were surprised that the Hudson family continued to live in this same house even after Jennifer became famous. Her family, especially her mother, did not want to leave their beloved home, their familiar neighborhood, their friends, or their church. Even with the demands placed on her time, with her busy schedule of filming, recording, touring, and promoting her many projects, Hudson returned often to visit her family home. Indeed, fame does not seem to have gone to the South Side native's head. The woman known to her fans as "JHud" laughingly told an interviewer in 2006, "I come home and I have to stand in line like everybody else."[2] She continued to visit her family frequently in Chicago after she became a celebrity, and as her cousin Krista Nichols-Alston noted, "When she comes in, she's just Jenny Gal. She's just Jennifer."[3]

The city Hudson grew up in has embraced her, as well. Chicago declared March 6, 2007, to be Jennifer Hudson Day. Her old high

Even after all her fame and success, Jennifer Hudson still calls South Side Chicago "home."

school, Dunbar Vocational Career Academy, has also honored her by creating a Jennifer Hudson Room, which is filled with *Dreamgirls* posters and mementos of Hudson's stint on *American Idol*. Hudson returned these favors during a December 2009 holiday special on ABC called *Jennifer Hudson: I'll Be Home for Christmas*. In the special, she refers to Chicago as the best place to be. "It is the greatest city in the world at Christmas,"[4] she declared.

It is no wonder that Hudson identifies so strongly with this remarkable city, for she is a remarkable woman. Much like Chicago rebounded after the Great Fire, she has bounced back from adversity and setbacks in her life. Her courage, resolve, and deep faith have helped her to remain strong when she has been faced with professional disappointment and personal tragedy.

Chapter 1

Humble Beginnings

When Jennifer Hudson was born, the last thing her family might have imagined she would become was a singer. Born with underdeveloped lungs, she was small for her age. She was also a very shy and emotional child who cried easily. In time, however, she overcame these obstacles. As she grew bigger, her lungs got stronger. Her family soon discovered that little Jennifer was drawn to the music she heard around her, in church as well as in her everyday life.

Music became one of Jennifer's greatest joys. She grew up in a home filled with music, in a family who all loved to sing, which strongly influenced her own desire to become a singer. It was a tight-knit family. Jennifer enjoyed a very close relationship with her mother (Darnell), stepfather (Samuel), brother (Jason), and sister (Julia), as well as the many cousins who lived nearby. One family member in particular, though, her grandmother (also named Julia), had an enormous influence on her. Jennifer's loving and deeply religious family helped shape her into the gracious and well-respected person she is today.

"We Had Everything We Needed"

Jennifer Kate Hudson was born on September 12, 1981, in Chicago, Illinois. She was the youngest child of Darnell Hudson, a single mother who worked as a secretary. Jennifer's biological father appears to have taken no part in her life, and no mention of him has been made in the media. When Jennifer was still quite young, however, her mother married Samuel Simpson, a bus driver. Although he was actually their stepfather, Jennifer and her siblings thought of him—and referred to him—as their father.

Jennifer grew up with two older siblings, Julia and Jason. They lived in a working-class neighborhood called Englewood, on the South Side of Chicago. The poverty and crime rates in Englewood are among the highest in Chicago. To Jennifer and her family, however, Englewood felt safe because it was home.

Even though the Hudsons were not wealthy, they were happy. Pictured Jennifer Hudson (C), sister Julia Hudson (L), mother Darnell Donerson (R) and nephew Julian King.

The family lived very modestly. Like the other families in their neighborhood, they did not have a lot of money. In spite of this, Darnell and Samuel were able to provide for their children and live relatively comfortably. Although their house was old and plain, it was very roomy, with two stories and nine bedrooms. Later, Jennifer looked back on her childhood and recalled, "We were poor but we thought we were rich, because we had everything we needed."[5]

Jennifer, her siblings, and her parents had a warm and loving home life. Both parents took active roles in the children's daily lives, providing the guidance and direction needed to keep their children safe and happy. Jennifer later described her mother's loving care: "I remember when my mom used to sit and bounce me on her knee. I used to itch a lot, and to put me to sleep she would have to scratch me. She had so much patience."[6]

The thing Jennifer recalls most about her family life is the music. The radio or stereo was always on, and her family members loved to sing, especially her mother and grandmother. The family also prayed together and discussed God and religion at home. In addition, they occasionally took trips around the United States when Jennifer was a child, attending family reunions and church functions. Always a sensitive child, Jennifer loved getting to know her extended family, and each relative held a special place in her heart.

"This Child Is Going to Sing"

The Hudson-Simpson family was a particularly religious one, and church was a very big part of their life. They attended Chicago's Pleasant Gift Missionary Baptist Church every week, sometimes twice a week. One of Jennifer's favorite parts about the service was the music, especially the singing.

Even as an infant, Jennifer's love of music was evident. One of the stories her mother most enjoyed telling others was about the time when eight-month-old Jennifer was in church during a choir practice. The choir was trying to hit a high note but could not quite reach it. Baby Jennifer, however, chimed in and hit the note perfectly. At that point, her godmother, Debra Nichols Windham, said to Darnell, "Mark my words, this child is going to sing."[7]

An important early influence on Jennifer's singing, as well as on her deep faith, was her maternal grandmother, Julia Kate Hudson. Some of Jennifer's earliest memories are of singing on her grandmother's knee at home. Her grandmother had a strong singing voice with a wide range, and Jennifer seemed to have inherited her talent and rich voice. Her grandmother, who sang in the soprano section of the church choir, also instilled in Jennifer a passion for singing and helped her overcome her shyness by encouraging her to sing at home and in church.

Jennifer's grandmother influenced her singing in other ways as well, first by serving as the young girl's music teacher. The two of them would sit together and take turns singing songs from the choir to each other. Before long, a seven-year-old Jennifer joined the soprano section and was singing alongside her grandmother in church. Together, they attended choir practice every Sunday and Tuesday.

"The Heart of Music"

By the time Jennifer joined the church choir, she already knew she wanted to be a singer when she grew up. She begged the choir director, the pastor, and the organist to let her sing solos, but they felt she was too young for such a responsibility. Jennifer later recalled sitting in the bathroom of her house as a young girl and crying because she was not given the solos she so longed for. She thought it was because no one wanted to hear her sing. In lieu of singing solos in front of others, she sang to herself in the bathroom. Even at that young age, Jennifer's determination to be a star was apparent: Her sister, Julia, recalled years later, "All Jennifer wanted to do was sing—and be famous."[8]

Jennifer's persistence and determination paid off when she was eventually given choir solos. Her first solo was the hymn "Must Jesus Bear the Cross Alone." Halfway through the song, however, she forgot the words. She managed to cover her embarrassment, and the mishap did not stop her from continuing to sing hymns at church. Despite this incident, she remained strong-willed and

Jennifer Hudson started singing in a church choir, like this one, at the young age of seven.

confident, displaying at a young age the traits that would serve her well as an adult.

Like the rest of her family, Jennifer was an avid churchgoer with a strong faith. The regular church services and choir practices helped to instill in her the values of hard work and clean living. Although her family lived in a rough neighborhood, Jennifer managed to stay clear of trouble. Growing up, she did not drink, smoke, or do drugs. "I never have and I never plan on it,"[9] she later told an interviewer.

Jennifer credits her involvement with the choir with some-

The Queen of Soul

One of Jennifer Hudson's favorite recording artists is Aretha Franklin, known as the Queen of Soul. Born in 1942 in a two-room house in Memphis, Tennessee, Franklin relocated with her family to Detroit, Michigan, at the age of six. The daughter of a Baptist minister, Franklin grew up singing in church, where she developed her gospel style and powerful singing voice.

Franklin's first big hit was a blues ballad titled "I Never Loved a Man (the Way I Love You)," released in 1967. The song reached number nine on the pop charts and

Aretha Franklin grew up singing in church, just like Jennifer Hudson.

number one on the rhythm and blues charts. Other top ten hits include "(You Make Me Feel Like) A Natural Woman" and "Chain of Fools," both released in 1967. Her biggest hit, which became her signature song, is the rhythm and blues classic "Respect," released in 1967. The song became associated with both the civil rights movement and the women's movement.

Franklin enjoyed a comeback in the 1980s, and in 1987 she became the first female artist to be inducted into the Rock and Roll Hall of Fame. She sang "God Bless America" at Barack Obama's presidential inauguration in 2009. Franklin, who is approaching her seventieth birthday, successfully underwent surgery for pancreatic cancer in late 2010.

thing else as well. Learning to sing in the church helped her to develop her belting, gospel style of singing. She says that church will always be her favorite place to sing, and she points out that many great singers got their start singing in church, just as she did. To her—and to many others, as well—singing in church provides a sense of meaning. And that, Jennifer says, is "the heart of music."[10]

The Girl's Got Soul

Even before Jennifer made up her mind to become a singer, she knew she wanted a job doing something creative. This ambition was inspired in part by her mother's encouragement of all her children's creativity through hobbies and extracurricular activities in the arts. Jennifer's brother, Jason, took piano lessons, and Jennifer studied ballet. She also had a chance to model, appearing in the catalog for the Chicago Sears at age five. Jennifer also explored her creative side by drawing and writing songs.

It was music, however, that interested Jennifer the most. In later years, she would give credit to her grandmother for inspiring her singing career. Yet another way in which her grandmother influenced her was by passing along her personal tastes in music. Jennifer has always liked listening to the artists that her grandmother and mother grew up listening to. Her favorite styles of music include rhythm and blues, gospel, and pop. As a child, Jennifer sang along with soul greats Aretha Franklin, Gladys Knight, and Patti LaBelle. She also liked listening to the music of gospel singers Mahalia Jackson, Shirley Caesar, Tramaine Hawkins, and Lucretia Campbell.

When Jennifer got a little older, her favorite artists included Whitney Houston, Celine Dion, and Destiny's Child. The first CD she ever bought was *Just the Beginning*, which was released in 1992 by the rhythm and blues group Voices and included the single "M.M.D.R.N.F. (My Mama Didn't Raise No Fool)." Her favorite songs to sing as a child and a teenager included "Inseparable" (Natalie Cole), "Neither One of Us" (Gladys Knight), and "I Believe in You and Me" (Whitney Houston).

Soul Train

Like Jennifer Hudson, the American musical variety show *Soul Train* got its start in Chicago. The show aired from 1971 to 2006 and featured music as well as dancing. The show was notable for providing viewers a window into African American culture. Young people, both black and white, tuned in for the latest styles in music, dance, and fashion.

During its thirty-five years on the air, *Soul Train* featured guest appearances by hundreds of well-known singers and celebrities. The show's guest list included Paula Abdul, Christina Aguilera, the Black Eyed Peas, Mary J. Blige, Mariah Carey, Sean Combs, Destiny's Child, Jamie Foxx, Aretha Franklin, Whitney Houston, Michael Jackson, Gladys Knight and the Pips, Patti LaBelle, Ludacris, OutKast, Queen Latifah, Usher, and hundreds of others. Each episode of *Soul Train* ended with the catch phrase "We wish you love, peace and soul!"

Quoted in Steve Jones. "It's the 'Sooouuuullll Train' Documentary! On VH1, Honey!" *USA Today*, February 7, 2010. www.usatoday.com/life/music/news/2010-02-05-soul-train05_ST_N.htm.

One of Jennifer's favorite television programs was *Soul Train*. This was a musical variety show that featured performances primarily of rhythm and blues, soul, hip-hop, and gospel artists. Funk, jazz, rock, disco, and rap artists have also appeared on the show. Jennifer especially liked the performances by the rhythm and blues, soul, and gospel singers.

A Promise for the Future

Jennifer's first public singing performance outside of church came when she was still a child and sang at her great-great-grandmother's ninety-first birthday party. Her family and friends who attended the party were impressed by the little girl's voice and told her it was a gift. Today, Jennifer says, "My voice is like a wonderful gift from God."[11]

Jennifer Hudson attended the Dunbar Vocational Career Academy, the same school that entertainers Lou Rawls and Mr. T (pictured) attended.

As Jennifer moved into high school, she discovered further opportunities to sing by attending the Dunbar Vocational Career Academy, a public school that focuses on preparing students to pursue various careers, including those in the arts. The academy counts among its alumni well-known performers such as Lawrence Tureaud (better known as Mr. T), Lou Rawls, and Cleotha and Pervis Staples of the Staple Singers. For Jennifer Hudson, too, the Dunbar Academy would lead to bigger and better things.

Although Jennifer did not date much in high school, her warm, friendly personality and good sense of humor made her well liked by the other students. She was also a favorite of her teachers and did well academically. She earned good grades and was on the honor roll her sophomore through senior years.

Once again, a family member would exert great influence over Jennifer's singing career. This time, it was her cousin Shari Nichols-Sweat, who was one of the music teachers at Dunbar. Jennifer later said of her, "She was definitely one of my role models. . . . She believed in me so much—it was like an amazing support system."[12] Nichols-Sweat was very impressed by the charismatic quality of Jennifer's voice and worked with her to develop it further. With the encouragement of her cousin, Jennifer joined the school's spirit choir. It was a decision that would change the course of her life.

Jennifer quickly became the star of her high school choir, performing in school musical productions. Her performances helped to make her very popular, and her classmates voted her the most talented female musician in school. Her choral teacher, Richard Nunley, was also impressed by her voice. He taught her classical singing techniques because he wanted her to develop her voice so she could sing any style of music she desired. Jennifer worked hard to master classical singing, and Nunley said later, "She's also a great classical singer, and a lot of people don't know that."[13]

It was while she was a student at Dunbar that Jennifer made a promise to both herself and her choral teacher. As Nunley recalled later, she told him on several different occasions, "I'm going to make you proud of me. I'm going to be a famous singer."[14]

Singing in the school's choir was only the beginning for Jennifer. More opportunities to explore and develop her singing voice would open up to her while she was still in high school. The love, support, and guidance of her extended family and her teachers while she was growing up helped Jennifer to overcome her childhood shyness and believe in her voice—and herself.

Chapter 2

Following Her Heart

Jennifer Hudson fully intended to fulfill the promise she made to her high school choral teacher, Richard Nunley. As she progressed through school, she became more and more certain she was meant to be a professional singer. Before she graduated from high school, however, another experience would fan her desire for fame.

From Burgers to Talent Competitions

When Jennifer was sixteen years old, she got a job at the Burger King restaurant at Eighty-Seventh and State Streets in Chicago. Her sister, Julia, worked there and had helped Jennifer get hired. Julia really liked her job there, so Jennifer expected she would too. She soon found, however, that the fast food environment was not to her liking. She hated the long, tedious hours in the restaurant. In addition, she felt like she was wasting what she had long thought of as her gift: her singing talent. Before long, Jennifer gave her notice to the restaurant manager and quit her job at Burger King.

Although her job in the fast food industry was short-lived, it was still a good experience for Jennifer. She learned that working at a menial job for minimum wage was not the kind of life she wanted. She was even more motivated to pursue her dream

Jennifer Hudson felt she was wasting her singing talent working at Burger King, so soon after she was hired, she quit.

of becoming an entertainer so that she could do something she loved for a living.

To this end, while she was still in high school, she began to perform outside of school and church. A childhood friend, Walter Williams, helped promote her around town. With Williams's help, Jennifer entered talent shows and performed in community musical productions. She sang at any and every event she could, just to get the experience and the exposure. She also performed in gay bars and drag clubs (where men dress up as women), although she was underage. At the same time, she continued to sing regularly in the choir, both at church and at school. As busy as she was with talent competitions and musical productions around town, she still managed to maintain a high grade point average. By the time she graduated from Dunbar Vocational Career Academy with honors in 1999, Jennifer Hudson had already gained a great deal of experience singing in public and was a regular on the local music scene.

Big Changes in Jennifer's Life

Around this same time, several significant events occurred in Hudson's personal life. She and the rest of her family were greatly saddened by the death of her beloved maternal grandmother, Julia Kate Hudson, in 1998. Julia had not only been Jennifer's mentor and first music teacher; she had also helped coach Jennifer for the talent shows and for her roles in the community musical productions while she was in high school.

Today, Hudson says she still thinks of her grandmother every time she sings. She views her powerful singing voice as a gift from her late grandmother, and she sees her career as a tribute to her. One of her grandmother's favorite songs to sing was "How Great Thou Art." Hudson keeps a recording in her iPod of African American gospel singer Mahalia Jackson singing this well-known hymn, and she thinks of her grandmother whenever she listens to the song. In addition, she says that she often thinks of her grandmother right before a performance in order to build up her emotions and to inspire herself. She says she knows how proud her grandmother would be of her and is motivated by the thought, "What if she could see me now?"[15]

The year after losing her grandmother, Hudson and her family suffered another loss when Samuel Simpson died of cancer. Although he was technically their stepfather, Hudson and her siblings always thought of him and referred to him as their father. Along with Darnell, Samuel had provided for the three kids a loving and supportive family environment.

On a brighter note, Hudson began a long-term relationship with James Payton in 1999. James, a maintenance engineer, was her brother's best friend, and she had known him since she was thirteen years old. They began dating around the time she graduated from high school, and the couple remained together for several years.

Another bright moment in Hudson's personal life came in

As a tribute to her grandmother, Hudson's mentor and first music teacher, Jennifer keeps the gospel song "How Great Thou Art" by Mahalia Jackson on her iPod. It was one of her grandmother's favorite songs, and Jennifer listens to it before she performs.

2001. That year, her sister, Julia, gave birth to a baby boy. Jennifer doted on her new nephew, who was named Julian in honor of his mother and great-grandmother.

Going to College and Going Pro

Soon after Hudson and Payton began dating, their relationship faced a challenge: they were separated from each other by several hundred miles. After graduating from high school, Hudson left Chicago for Langston, Oklahoma. There, she attended Langston University, a historically black university that has one of the top choral programs in the nation. Always a good student, she enjoyed attending her classes. Yet Hudson was not entirely happy at Langston. It was her first time so far away from home, and she was terribly homesick. She missed her family and her boyfriend. In addition, Langston is a rural town, which is very different from urban Chicago.

To be closer to home, she decided to transfer to Kennedy-King College, a two-year community college in Chicago. At college, Hudson took some general music classes but chose not to major in music because she believed teaching was the only career a degree in music would allow, and she did not want to be a music teacher. In fact, she was more interested in the art classes that she took, in part because she had always liked drawing.

While attending Kennedy-King, Hudson began performing professionally for the first time. She soon became an in-demand paid singer at various clubs and at functions around town, including weddings, birthday parties, and graduations. She also sang at her uncle's funeral parlor for people's funerals. During college, she thought that if her career as a singer did not work out, she might like to work at the funeral home—but as a mortician.

Jennifer's Big Break

As it turned out, becoming a mortician was a short-lived idea that was eclipsed by an opportunity Hudson had been dreaming of since she was a child. In January 2001, while still attending Kennedy-King College, she auditioned for a part in a musical that was to play at Chicago's Marriott Lincolnshire Theatre, one of the city's professional regional theaters. The musical was *Big River*, written

Jennifer's first big break came with a part in Big River, a musical based on the Mark Twain novel Adventures of Huckleberry Finn.

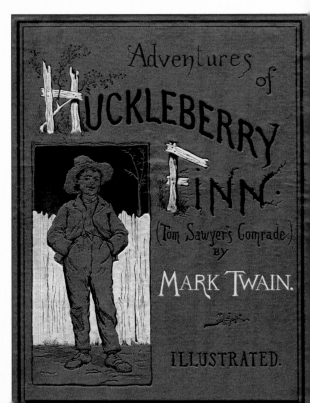

by country-pop singer and songwriter Roger Miller. *Big River* was originally performed on Broadway and had won a Tony Award for Best Musical in 1985. It is based on Mark Twain's 1884 novel, *Adventures of Huckleberry Finn,* which is often referred to as the "great American novel." Twain's classic is set in various places along the Mississippi River and depicts aspects of society in the South before the Civil War—most particularly, the relationships between blacks and whites. The setting of the novel is reflected in the bluegrass- and country-style music in *Big River.*

Hudson was thrilled to learn she had passed her audition and was cast as a singer and actor in the musical. Her belting, bluesy voice was well suited to the production's musical style. Although she had only a small singing part with no spoken lines, the role provided her with both professional stage experience and acting credentials. Hudson later described the experience as a defining moment for her: "That's when I knew I could actually make a living doing this."[16]

That realization led to an important decision for Hudson. Landing a role in *Big River* was the kind of opportunity she had dreamed of since she was a little girl. So she decided to leave college and instead pursue her career as a singer and an actress. Hudson later said in an interview with *Essence* magazine, "I don't actually consider myself a college dropout, I consider myself a college fugitive." She explained that she saw college as a road to a career, and that when this opportunity to be in a musical presented itself, "I believed in myself and went for it."[17] Hudson was now able to focus entirely on her career, and she stayed with the production of *Big River* for its entire run of nearly two years.

Singing on the High Seas

Big River was a wonderful experience for Hudson. It gave her a taste of what life as a professional singer was like. So, as the production neared its final days, Hudson looked around for another musical in which she could showcase and further develop her singing talent. She found such an opportunity with the Disney Cruise Line.

The Disney Cruise Line

The Disney Cruise Line is owned and operated by Walt Disney Parks and Resorts, a division of the Walt Disney Company, and is headquartered in Celebration, Florida. Created in 1995, the cruise line consists of four ships: the *Disney Magic* and the *Disney Wonder,* in service during Hudson's time as a cast member, the *Disney Dream,* christened in 2011, and the *Disney Fantasy,* scheduled to join the line in 2012. Each of the family-friendly ships contains nine hundred staterooms and has special areas for different age groups, including young children, teenagers, and adults. There are many differences in the way the ships are decorated, however. The *Disney Magic,* for example, features the figure of Sorcerer Mickey at the bow (front of the boat) and a painting of Goofy at the stern (rear of the boat). The interior of the ship is decorated in art deco style, with sleek, modern lines. The *Disney Wonder,* aboard which Jennifer Hudson sailed in 2003, has a figure of Steamboat Willie at the bow and a painting of Donald Duck and his nephew Huey on the stern. The interior of the ship is decorated in an art nouveau style, with fanciful, swirling wave designs. The statues in each lobby are also different: The *Disney Magic* features Helmsman Mickey, and the *Disney Wonder* features Ariel from *The Little Mermaid.*

Operated by a division of the Walt Disney Company, the cruise line included two ships at the time, the *Disney Magic* and the *Disney Wonder.* In the fall of 2002, Hudson auditioned for a show that was to be performed aboard the *Disney Wonder, Hercules: The Musical,* based on the 1997 Disney movie *Hercules.* After her audition, Hudson was awarded her first major role, that of Calliope. Calliope is the narrator and the head muse, or source of inspiration, of the character Hercules.

From February through July 2003, Hudson sailed the Bahamas on the *Disney Wonder* and performed as Calliope in the ship's musical. Performing on a ship posed certain unique challenges, as Hudson soon discovered. Keeping her balance on a moving ship while in a costume that included very high heels and a huge wig took some getting used to. The constant motion, and commotion, of living aboard a ten-deck floating city with more than thirty-three hundred passengers and crew also took some adjusting to, even when she was not in costume. She persevered, however, and entertained aboard the *Disney Wonder* for six months. During that time, she thought of herself as part of the "Disney family," which helped her to cope with missing her own, tight-knit family back in Chicago. She loved the live performances and found it thrilling to be able to sing in front of thousands of people—and to be paid to do it.

An Influential Role Model

Hudson had always been a fan of popular music, and she enjoyed listening to the latest hit songs. During the time she sailed the Bahamas on the *Disney Wonder,* she began to take notice of several new songs, as well as the artists performing them. This period of her life would prove to be a pivotal one.

In the summer of 2003, a singer from one of Hudson's favorite groups, Destiny's Child, released her debut solo album. Titled *Dangerously in Love*, the album by Beyoncé Knowles produced the number one hits "Crazy in Love" and "Baby Boy." Hudson loved to sing along with these hit songs, and the album soon became her favorite. She also took note of Knowles's burgeoning career as both a singer and an actress. Hudson greatly admired and respected Knowles's talent and success, and wanted a similar career for herself. As Hudson boldly put it, "I believe in myself, and I want to do it all. I plan to model, put on an album, do Broadway, design greeting cards. I see myself becoming like Beyoncé—who is marvelous—only three times more successful."[18]

Hudson was also closely following the careers of several new artists, among them Kelly Clarkson, Ruben Studdard, and Clay Aiken. Clarkson released her debut album, *Thankful*, in the spring of 2003. The album spawned several hit songs and went on to sell 4.5 million copies worldwide. Studdard released his first single, "Flying Without Wings," in the summer of 2003,

Beyoncé Knowles

One of the artists Jennifer Hudson most wanted to emulate was singer, songwriter, actress, and fashion designer Beyoncé Knowles. Born in Houston, Texas, in 1981—the same year as Hudson—Knowles entered many singing and dancing competitions at a young age. She gained widespread fame with the formation of the rhythm and blues girl group Destiny's Child in the late 1990s. As the lead singer, Knowles helped the group become one of the top-selling girl groups in music history. In 2003 Knowles released the solo album *Dangerously in Love,* which won five Grammy Awards. In 2006 she released *B'Day,* which debuted at number one on the Billboard charts and won a Grammy for Best Contemporary R&B album. Her third album, *I Am ... Sasha Fierce,* released in 2008, included the smash-hit "Single Ladies (Put a Ring on It)." This album earned Knowles a record-breaking six Grammy Awards. With a total of sixteen Grammys, Knowles is the third-most-honored female artist of all time.

Knowles branched out to acting in 2001 in the musical film *Carmen: A Hip Hopera*, followed by *Austin Powers in Goldmember* in 2002. In 2004 she entered the world of fashion design when she launched House of Deréon along with her mother, stylist and designer Tina Knowles.

Beyoncé Knowles walks the runway at the Fashion for Relief fashion show, with proceeds going to aid Hurricane Katrina victims, during Olympus Fashion Week at Bryant Park September 16, 2005, in New York City.

Jennifer was closely following the careers of American Idol winners (L-R) Ruben Studdard, Kelly Clarkson, and Clay Aiken, as she considered her future career.

and the song reached the number two spot on the *Billboard* Hot 100 chart. The number one spot on the chart was held by "This Is the Night," which was the debut single of Clay Aiken and was also released in the summer of 2003. These three talented new singers had something else in common aside from their simultaneous successes—all three had been contestants on the hit reality TV show *American Idol.* This fact did not escape Hudson's attention as she considered her future after *Hercules: The Musical.*

Keeping Her Balance

When Hudson's first contract with the Disney Cruise Line expired, the company offered her a second contract. Hudson, however, made a decision that turned out to be a monumental career move. She turned down the second contract with Disney to try out for the biggest talent competition in the country: *American Idol.*

It was actually Hudson's mother who first suggested that she try out for *Idol.* Darnell knew the show would give Jennifer more exposure than she had had so far, and a much bigger audience than the cruise ship. Hudson was eager for the opportunity to sing on national television. In addition, the winner of the competition

would get a recording contract with a major label—something Hudson had dreamed of since she was a little girl, listening to Aretha Franklin, Gladys Knight, and other great singers with her grandmother.

Hudson's experiences in *Big River* and on the Disney cruise ship, as well as all her previous singing gigs in clubs and for church and social functions, had helped her to hone a powerful six-octave singing voice. This amazing vocal range—the ability to sing notes from the lowest (called chest notes) to the highest (called whistle notes) the human voice can produce—is extremely rare. In addition, by this time she had several years of professional experience singing in front of live audiences and had developed a charming and charismatic stage presence. Hudson believed she had what it takes to become the next *American Idol*. As she told an interviewer, if she could keep her balance while performing on the *Disney Wonder* all those months, that proved something about her stamina and determination: "'If I can get through the ship, that means I'm cut out for *Idol*."[19]

Chapter 3

Stepping into the Spotlight on *American Idol*

Jennifer Hudson knew that the winner of the third season of American Idol would receive a $1 million recording contract with RCA. But winning the fierce competition was a significant long shot. At twenty-two years old, Hudson had only her experience in local theater and on the Disney cruise ship to fall back on. She had no formal training in singing. What she had, however, was a powerful voice and a deep determination to pursue a career as a singer. With the encouragement and support of her family, Hudson flew to Atlanta, Georgia, in August 2003 to audition for *American Idol*.

Hudson's Big Audition

Hudson's *American Idol* audition was the first exciting step in a journey that would transform her life. There were eleven thousand people auditioning in six different cities around the country for the show's third season. When she arrived in Atlanta, some of the thousands of hopefuls there had been waiting outside the Georgia Dome for two days for their big chance. The first hurdle was to sing for the show's producers, who screened contestants before they faced *American Idol*'s three judges: Simon Cowell, Paula Abdul, and Randy Jackson. Hudson passed this initial screening and was ready to appear before the judges.

As her audition began, Jackson told her that they expected her to give a better job in the audition than "a cruise ship performance." Hudson, wearing a little black dress for the occasion, assured him she would. She then sang "Share Your Love with Me," which was originally recorded by Aretha Franklin. Jackson said of her audition: "absolutely brilliant, the best singer I've heard so far."[20] Abdul agreed that Hudson's voice was excellent, and Cowell made the decision unanimous. Afterward, Hudson burst through the stage doors singing her announcement to her family that she was going to Hollywood.

Facing Criticism from the Judges

Before reaching Hollywood, however, Hudson had to survive another round of auditions held in Pasadena, California. Hudson flew there with the other 116 contestants from all over the nation who had passed the initial audition. The contestants spent a week practicing and auditioning; only thirty-two of them would make the cut this time around.

During this round of auditions, Hudson received some criticism from the judges. First, Cowell criticized her outfit, an unflattering, too-tight silver jumper. He told her she looked like "something you'd wrap a turkey in"[21] and that she was lucky she was not being judged on her wardrobe. The other judges kept their comments focused on her singing, but these, too, were critical in nature. Abdul, for example, said it sounded like Hudson was shouting rather than singing.

It was not the last time that the judges would negatively critique Hudson, sometimes quite harshly, on both her appearance and the quality of her voice. On another occasion, Cowell told her she was out of her league and did not measure up to the other contestants. Rather than giving up, however, Hudson reacted in a way that is typical of her. Cowell's comment did not make her feel humiliated, as she later explained to journalist Barbara Walters. "If anything, I felt challenged,"[22] Hudson said.

Jennifer Hudson competed against 116 other Hollywood week finalists to earn a spot on **American Idol,** *Season 3.*

Hudson Goes to Hollywood

In spite of some pointed criticism, Hudson made it through the auditions in Pasadena to become one of the top thirty-two contestants who went on to Hollywood. There, she was supported every week by a loving crowd of friends and family, which at various times included her mother, brother, sister, cousins, and boyfriend, James Payton.

As the show progressed week after week, Hudson showed her ability to rise above the judges' sometimes harsh words with grace and style. On the February 10, 2004, broadcast, she had a comeback to Cowell's earlier wardrobe insult. After she finished singing "Imagine," which was originally recorded by John Lennon, she coyly asked Cowell if he liked her outfit that night. She was wearing a white dress with white boots. He smiled and said that he did, but then made a joke about her wearing a leather nurse's outfit. Hudson humorously shot back that Cowell had better not end up at her hospital.

Her lighthearted exchange with Cowell aside, Hudson endured some mild criticism from Jackson that night. He commented that he "wasn't blown away"[23] by her singing in that round. Hudson took his words in stride, nodding politely. When Abdul observed that Hudson seemed more reserved than usual that night, Hudson replied that she was feeling quite emotional. As she spoke, she was moved to tears, which visibly touched the judges. Later, in the Red Room, where the contestants were interviewed after performing, Hudson told host Ryan Seacrest that she was so emotional because she felt overjoyed to be on the show. She explained, "My dream has always been for the world to hear me sing one time, and this was the second or third, so this is an unbelievable blessing."[24]

Unfortunately for Hudson, in spite of the judges' generally positive response to her performance that night, she was eliminated. The judges did not think her singing was good enough for her to continue, and they voted her off the show during the semifinals. She returned to Chicago with her mother and sister, who had been in the audience watching her perform that night. But it would not be the last time that America would hear her sing.

A Wild Card for Hudson

Hudson thought that it was all over for her on *American Idol*. Then she got unexpected good news: She was being invited back to the show for the wild card round. In this round, eight contestants who were eliminated earlier would be brought back for a chance to become a finalist on the show. The three judges would pick one contestant each, and the viewers would choose a fourth. These four would join the remaining eight original contestants to make twelve finalists in all.

Randy, Paula, and Simon

American Idol has featured a variety of judges over the years, but three are most closely identified with the show: Randy Jackson, Paula Abdul, and Simon Cowell.

Jackson is a former session singer and bassist who has recorded with several prominent artists, including Carlos Santana, Aretha Franklin, and Madonna. He is also a record producer and music manager who has worked with Mariah Carey, Whitney Houston, Fergie, and others.

Former Los Angeles Lakers cheerleader Paula Abdul started out in show business as a choreographer, most notably for Janet Jackson. In 1988 Abdul released an album of her own titled *Forever Your Girl,* which produced four number one hit singles. Two more albums followed: the Triple Platinum *Spellbound* in 1991 and her final album, *Head over Heels,* in 1995.

British-born Simon Cowell got his start in the mailroom of EMI Music Publishing before becoming a successful music manager and executive. Cowell appeared as a judge on the British TV series *Pop Idol* and later on the show's American version, *American Idol,* which premiered June 11, 2002. He became well known on both shows for his blunt, harsh criticisms of contestants.

As of 2011, only Jackson remained of the three original judges on *Idol.* Abdul announced in August 2009 that she would not be returning for the ninth season. Then in January 2010, Cowell announced that he would leave the show at the end of that season.

The three judges of American Idol, Season 3, (L-R) Simon Cowell, Paula Abdul, and Randy Jackson.

Even though Jennifer was chosen for the wild card round, the criticism of her personal style continued.

Hudson was very excited to get another chance. During the wild card round, broadcast on March 9, she was the last singer to perform. She sang Whitney Houston's "I Believe in You and Me." Afterward, she received both praise and criticism from the judges. Jackson told her it was the best performance that night, but said he did not like her outfit—she was wearing a strapless, form-fitting pink dress that did not flatter her curvy figure. Cowell, too, said he did not like her outfit and added that she should fire her dressmaker, calling the dress "hideous."[25] He also said that she needed to develop more control over her voice. Abdul had only good things to say, and she paid a compliment that meant a lot to Hudson: "You have this muscle in your voice that you flex, and you tell a story with the song. You convey a story and it moves and touches every single one of us."[26]

Then it was time for the judges to announce their wild card choices. Jackson spoke first, keeping the contestants in suspense while he explained that he had put a lot of thought into his decision. At last, he announced that his choice was Jennifer Hudson. She was overjoyed to be brought back to the show as a finalist. Yet even at that joyous moment, she had to endure yet another criticism of her appearance; Cowell told her she needed to find a stylist she could see, a reference to her bushy hair that partially covered her eyes.

"Everything About You Is Too Much"

Hudson was at last one of the final twelve. From here on out, her fate—and that of the other contestants—would be decided by votes from the reality show's viewers, rather than the judges. Each night the show aired, viewers called a toll-free number to vote for their favorite performer; the performer with the fewest votes on each show would be eliminated one by one.

During this stage of the competition, criticisms of Hudson's singing and appearance continued. After her performance of "Baby, I Love You," which had been made popular by Aretha Franklin, Cowell warned Hudson that if she did not stop over-singing (when a singer pushes her voice too far and winds up off-key), viewers would tire of her. Another night, Abdul complained that Hudson seemed to be holding back in her performance, and Cowell said Hudson was out of her league. As she later told an interviewer, "The *Idol* judges told me, 'Everything about you is too much. Your voice is too much. Your look is too much. Your hair is too much.'"[27]

It was not only the *Idol* judges that offered Hudson such criticism. Feedback from viewers on her performances came in the form of low votes during several shows. In fact, during one show, Hudson was in the bottom two. The other contestant in the bottom two, Leah LaBelle, was the one eliminated that night, but it had been a close call for Hudson. Negative comments about her fashion sense appeared in newspapers, magazines, and online chat rooms as well. For example, one writer for the *New York Times* said of her wide pink headband, "Is that a butterfly in her hair?"[28] Hudson responded to the many criticisms of her physical image by getting a makeover from the show's hair, makeup, and wardrobe staff. She replaced her previous, free-spirited outfits with tailored pantsuits, traded in her bushy hairstyle for one that was sleeker, and toned down her dramatic makeup.

During these rounds of the show, Hudson earned a nickname that included two other contestants, Fantasia Barrino and LaToya London. Together, the three women, all of whom are black and have similar voices and singing styles, became known as the "three divas." Because the term *diva* is often applied to a person who is talented but also conceited and demanding, Hudson did not care for the nickname. She tried to view it as a compliment that brought her and the other two women a lot of positive attention, rather than seeing the nickname as an insult.

A Shocking Revelation

By round four of the finals, the contestants had been narrowed down to the final nine. That week's show featured the music of singer and songwriter Elton John, who spent the entire week rehearsing with the contestants. Hudson chose to sing "Circle of

After Jennifer Hudson (R) gave a stellar performance, many were shocked that she was in the bottom three, along with Fantasia Barrino (L) and LaToya London (C), and then voted off American Idol.

Life" from the Disney animated movie *The Lion King*. After one rehearsal of the song, John said that Hudson had an astonishing voice and that listening to her sing gave him chills. The judges also praised Hudson after she performed the song during show. Jackson said it was the best performance of the night, as well as the best performance Hudson had given during the season. Abdul complimented Hudson for no longer holding back and for letting her true self shine through. Speaking last, Cowell told her that with that night's performance, she had finally proved that she deserved to be a finalist. It seemed that the harsh criticism was behind her.

In round six of the finals, the show was to feature the music of singer and songwriter Barry Manilow, who also spent a week rehearsing with contestants. Hudson performed Manilow's "Weekend in New England." During rehearsals, Manilow com-

The Other "Divas"

After Jennifer Hudson was voted off American Idol, two of the "three divas" still remained: LaToya London and Fantasia Barrino. Both women achieved success after the show. Fourth-place-finisher London released her debut album, *Love & Life,* in September 2005. The album, a mix of rhythm and blues, soul, jazz, and hip-hop, did not do very well on the charts and only sold about fifty-eight thousand copies. London found more success onstage, beginning in 2006 with the touring play *Issues: We All Have 'Em.* In 2007 to 2010, she earned rave reviews for her performance in the national tour of the Broadway musical *The Color Purple.*

Season 3 winner Barrino released her debut album, *Free Yourself,* in November 2004. The album earned Barrino four Grammy nominations. In 2006 she released her second album, *Fantasia,* which received three Grammy nominations. Like London, Barrino appeared in the Broadway musical *The Color Purple.* In addition, she sang a Grammy-nominated duet with Jennifer Hudson titled "I'm His Only Woman." Barrino's latest album, *Back to Me,* was released in 2010 and became her highest charting album, reaching number one on the *Billboard* R&B/Hip-Hop chart.

mented that Hudson's singing was so good that "it goes to another place."[29] After her performance on the April 21 show, Jackson told her, "That was unbelievable—you just get better every week."[30] The other two judges also raved about her performance.

With all that high praise, it came as a complete shock when Hudson finished in the bottom three that night, along with London and Barrino. Then it was revealed that Hudson had received the fewest number of call-in votes. She was eliminated from the show, finishing in seventh place. The studio audience, the contestants, and even the judges were shocked by the announcement. Hudson looked numb. The studio audience remained silent, and some of the contestants began to cry. Barrino threw her arms around Hudson and proclaimed in a voice choked with emotion, "You are my American Idol!"[31] Barrino—who went on to win that season—later revealed that she was upset by the outcome of that night's vote: "I was really angry when she got voted off."[32]

A Voting Controversy

Hudson's final elimination was the result of one of the closest votes in the show's history, and it sparked a controversy over the show's voting system. Elton John called that night's voting "incredibly racist."[33] He went on to explain that three of the performers he thought were very talented— and who also happened to be black—kept finishing in the bottom three in the voting. It was not only John who made this observation. The *New York Post,* which is owned by the same company that owns *American Idol* sponsor the Fox network, was flooded with calls from people who wanted the paper to investigate complaints of racially motivated voting.

A few other theories circulated for why the votes turned out the way they did that night. One theory is based on the fact that there was a series of windstorms and tornadoes that night in the area around Chicago—Hudson's hometown—and fifteen thousand homes lost power and telephone service. It was possible, Hudson fans suggested, that thousands of people in Chicago who could have been trying to call in to vote for Hudson were unable to get through. Another theory is that Hudson, Barrino, and London were simply the victims of the phenomenon known as vote splitting: Because these three contestants were so similar, callers who liked that singing style best split their votes three ways, with the result that no one of the three got a clear majority of votes. This idea helps explain why the three women kept receiving a low number of votes.

After Hudson's elimination, there were calls to change the way the show's voting is handled. Some people wanted the network to make the results of the voting public, so that the number of votes received by each contestant is clear. Others proposed the network find a way to limit the number of times that a person can call in and vote. The controversy over the show's voting system did not change anything for Hudson as she left *American Idol* and headed back to Chicago.

"Know That You Are a Star"

Despite coming in seventh place, Hudson's appearance on *American Idol* had drawn national attention. She remained calm and focused after her elimination, as she explained later: "I just knew I was going somewhere and I had to sing my way to it. And I couldn't give up."[34] She remained grateful for the experience and the exposure that *American Idol* brought her. Sooner than she imagined, her appearance on the show led to bigger and better opportunities.

Immediately after her final elimination, she made several TV appearances. She went on *Entertainment Tonight* and several talk shows. She also appeared on *The Late Show with David Letterman* and read "The Top 10 Things I Can Say Now That

After American Idol, Jennifer had many public appearances, including the American Idol Live! tour.

I've Lost American Idol." A compilation CD titled *American Idol Season 3: Greatest Soul Classics,* which included one song from each of the twelve finalists, was released in the spring of 2004. Hudson contributed the song "Neither One of Us (Wants to Be the First to Say Goodbye)," made popular by Gladys Knight and the Pips. Hudson also toured the United States with the American Idol Live! tour in the summer of 2004, singing songs by Aretha Franklin, Prince, and Beyoncé Knowles. At the end of the tour, Hudson returned home, where she was very much sought after as a performer around Chicago.

Her experiences on *American Idol* taught Hudson the importance of hard work and perseverance, lessons that would come in handy as she continued her professional journey. As for being eliminated from the show, Hudson had some words of advice to future *Idol* contestants. She cautioned them not to let criticism get to them and also not to let anyone intimidate them. "Believe in yourself and know that you are a star,"[35] Hudson says. It is perhaps this attitude that helped her to remain strong through all the ups and downs of her experience on *American Idol* and to not let her final elimination discourage her from pursuing a career as a singer.

Chapter 4

Dreams Come True

Despite her very painful and public rejection on national television, Jennifer Hudson did not give up on her dream of securing a recording contract with a major record label. When she returned to Chicago in the summer of 2004 after the American Idol Live! tour ended, she felt certain she would be offered a recording contract. She was disappointed and frustrated, however, when the offers did not come pouring in. In lieu of a contract, she went back to singing at weddings and nightclubs around Chicago. This was a big frustration and let-down for her, after having been a star on the most popular show on TV only a few months before.

Hudson found other work in addition to her local performances. In September 2004, for example, she appeared on Broadway in the rock musical *Hair*, alongside Wayne Brady, Michael McKean, RuPaul, and dozens of other performers. This one-night charity production was put on by the Actors Fund of America, a non-profit group that helps provide for the welfare of all entertainment professionals. The musical, which is set during the Vietnam War era, originally played on Broadway in 1967.

After her appearance in *Hair*, and still with no recording contract in sight, Hudson tried to produce an album independently. She spent about a year working on this project but went in a different direction in the fall of 2005 when she heard about open auditions for a movie that intrigued her.

A Dream Role

The movie was *Dreamgirls*, the film adaptation of the hit Broadway musical of the same name. The play opened on Broadway in 1981 and ran for more than fifteen hundred performances, picking up six Tony Awards along the way. *Dreamgirls* was adapted for the screen by screenwriter and director Bill Condon. It tells the story of the rise of an all-girl singing group called the Dreamettes in the 1960s and 1970s. The Dreamettes were a fictional group whose story is closely based on the real-life all-girl group the Supremes.

Hudson decided to audition for the part of Effie White, the lead singer of the Dreamettes who is replaced by a singer with a weaker voice but more slender figure. It was a major role and would require a considerable amount of acting in addition to singing. The twenty-five-year-old Hudson had minimal experience acting onstage in *Big River, Hercules,* and *Hair.* Those roles had been primarily singing parts, with only one or two lines of

Jennifer Hudson found work after her elimination from American Idol in the rock musical Hair, performed as a charity production by the Actors Fund of America.

The "Real" Effie White

The character Jennifer Hudson played in *Dreamgirls* is based on the real-life former singer of the Supremes, Florence Ballard. Along with childhood friends Diana Ross and Mary Wilson, the Detroit-born Ballard formed a group called the Supremes. In 1964 the three women signed a deal with Motown Records. Originally, Ballard was considered the lead singer, but she was gradually replaced in this role by Ross, whom the record producers thought was prettier and more likely to appeal to white audiences than Ballard. In 1967 the group's name was changed to Diana Ross and the Supremes, after which Ballard began missing public appearances and recording sessions. She was soon fired. Her attempt at a solo career in the late 1960s was unsuccessful, and she sank into a spiral of alcohol, poverty, and depression. Ballard remained largely forgotten by the public until a story about her misfortunes appeared in national newspapers in 1974. She enjoyed a brief comeback before her sudden death in 1976 from a blood clot near her heart. Hudson mentioned Ballard when accepting a Golden Globe for *Dreamgirls*, saying, "I want to dedicate this award to a lady who never got a fair chance, Florence Ballard. You will never be forgotten."

Jennifer Hudson acceptance speech, *64th Annual Golden Globe Awards*, NBC, January 15, 2007.

The Supremes L-R, Diana Ross, Mary Wilson, Florence Ballard

speaking. Still, Hudson was determined to win the role of Effie and prove she could act as well as sing.

She was up against very stiff competition for the role. There were 782 women auditioning for the part—including *American Idol* winner Fantasia Barrino. For her audition, Hudson sang "Easy to Be Hard," which she had performed in *Hair*. Then, she had to wait three months to find out whether she would be called back for a second audition. Just when she thought she would never hear from the movie's producers again, a casting agent called and asked her to read for the part in person. Much like the audition process for *American Idol,* the casting process for *Dreamgirls* turned into an emotional roller coaster. The movie's director and producers were concerned about her lack of acting experience. Over the next six months, Hudson auditioned two more times in New York. During this time, she went from being sure she had gotten the part to being told that she was not even being considered for the part anymore. At last, she was asked to do a screen test in Los Angeles, and two days later the director, Condon, called to tell her that the role of Effie White was hers.

It was the role of a lifetime for Hudson. She was about to star in a major motion picture along with a big-name cast that included Jamie Foxx, Eddie Murphy, Danny Glover, and Ankia Noni Rose. Perhaps most exciting of all, the movie starred one of her favorite singers and her personal idol, Beyoncé Knowles.

Blowing the Audience Away

When *Dreamgirls* premiered in December 2006, moviegoers were immediately taken by Hudson's debut performance. She had an easy, natural acting ability, and viewers identified with the raw emotion and vulnerability she conveyed in her portrayal of Effie. So powerful was her rendition of the six-octave "And I Am Telling You I'm Not Going" that audiences could not contain their enthusiasm for her performance. "It's not often that a movie audience breaks into spontaneous applause,"[36] points out movie critic Roger Ebert. Yet that is exactly what happened in theaters across America.

Hudson's (R) performance as Effie White in the Broadway musical–based film Dreamgirls *was so moving that at times, moviegoers would applaud during the film.*

In his review of the movie, Peter Travers of *Rolling Stone* magazine referred to Hudson as "a blazing new star." Travers added, "She can act. . . . And she can sing until the roof comes off the multiplex."[37] Viewers and critics alike thought that Hudson had outperformed pop star Beyoncé Knowles. During a guest appearance on *The Late Show with David Letterman*, Letterman said to Hudson: "They put you in this movie, which is a wonderful story, and incredibly talented people, and you come in and you steal the whole movie—your first time out!"[38]

Hudson's performance in *Dreamgirls* garnered her a total of thirty-six award nominations. Of these, she won thirty. Her awards as best supporting actress include a Golden Globe Award, a BAFTA Award, an NAACP Image Award, and a Screen Actors Guild Award. When she was nominated for the most prestigious of all awards, the Academy Award for Best Supporting Actress, Hudson summed up her feelings about the avalanche of accolades she was receiving: "I'm in shock. I'm overwhelmed. … It's unbelievable."[39]

Hudson went on to win the Oscar, becoming one of only a handful of actors to win the award for a debut screen performance. With her mother in the audience the night of the awards show, Hudson gave an emotional acceptance speech. "Oh my God, I have to just take this moment in," she said through tears. "I cannot believe this. Look what God can do. I didn't think I was going to win. If my grandmother was here to see me now. She was my biggest inspiration."[40] Hudson ended her acceptance speech by thanking Jennifer Holliday, the Tony Award–winning actress who had originally played the role of Effie White on Broadway.

In the Spotlight

In addition to the numerous acting awards, Hudson received attention for her version of the song "And I Am Telling You I'm Not Going." The song was released as a single, debuting at number 98 on the *Billboard* Hot 100 in January 2007. One month later, the song became a top 10 hit on the *Billboard* Hot Adult R&B Airplay chart. It also reached number 14 on the *Billboard* Hot R&B/Hip-Hop Songs chart.

The song had another benefit for Hudson as well. After music industry executive Clive Davis saw Hudson's screen test for the movie, in which she sang "And I Am Telling You I'm Not Going," he immediately offered her a contract with Arista Records. Davis was a legendary record producer who worked with artists such as Kelly Clarkson, Alicia Keys, Carlos Santana, Barry Manilow, and another of Hudson's personal idols, Whitney Houston.

In September 2008, Hudson released her debut album, *Jennifer Hudson*. The self-titled album, which debuted at number two on the *Billboard* 200 chart, was a collection of soul, rhythm and blues, and pop. The first single, a ballad titled "Spotlight," went to number one on the *Billboard* Hot R&B/Hip-Hop Songs chart. In all, the successful album produced five singles and three music videos. *Jennifer Hudson*, which sold more than 800,000 copies worldwide, was certified Gold by the Recording Industry Association of America. It was also nominated for four Grammy Awards and won the Grammy for best rhythm and blues album.

Kicking It into High Gear

Hudson's tremendous success in *Dreamgirls*, as well as the success of her debut album, helped kick her career into high gear. In the months following the movie's release, she made numerous TV appearances, including interviews on *Oprah* and *The Late Show with David Letterman*. She also appeared on the covers of several magazines, and in 2007 became the first African American singer and only the third African American celebrity to appear on the cover of *Vogue* (after Halle Berry and Oprah Winfrey).

In 2008, the same year her album was released, Hudson appeared in two other movies, neither of which revolved around singing. The first of these was *Sex and the City* (2008). The movie was based on the hit HBO TV series that ran from 1998 to 2004, which in turn was based on the novel *Sex and the City* by Candace Bushnell. Hudson played the part of Louise, the assistant to Carrie Bradshaw, who was played by Sarah Jessica Parker both on TV and in the movie. Hudson also sang the song "All Dressed in Love" on the movie's soundtrack, which debuted at number two on the *Billboard* 200. The movie was a financial success, becoming the year's top-grossing romantic comedy.

Sex and the City garnered mixed reviews from critics. A reviewer for the *New York Times* referred to it as "vulgar, shrill, deeply shallow."[41] Several publications, including the *London Times*, the *Daily Telegraph,* and the *New York Observer,* featured *Sex and the City* on their list of the year's worst movies. A reviewer for *Newsweek*, however, called the movie "incredibly sweet and touching,"[42] and the *Los Angeles Times* called Hudson's performance as Louise "likeable."[43]

Hudson's second film of 2008 was *The Secret Life of Bees,* which

Hudson co-starred with Dakota Fanning in The Secret Life of Bees, *which opened to mixed reviews.*

Queen Latifah

The rapper, actress, and singer known as Queen Latifah, who costarred in *The Secret Life of Bees* along with Jennifer Hudson, was born Dana Elaine Owens in Newark, New Jersey, in 1970. She first gained attention as a hip-hop artist when her debut album, *All Hail the Queen,* was released in 1989. The album reached number six on the Billboard Top R&B/ Hip-Hop Albums chart. In 1995 Latifah won a Grammy Award for Best Solo Rap Performance for her single "U.N.I.T.Y." She has received six other Grammy nominations.

Latifah made two guest appearances on the NBC sitcom *The Fresh Prince of Bel-Air,* which ran from 1990 to 1996 and starred fellow rapper Will Smith. She starred in her own sitcom, *Living Single,* on Fox from 1993 to 1998. She also had her own talk show, *The Queen Latifah Show*, from 1999 to 2001. Her first movie appearance was in Spike Lee's *Jungle Fever* (1991). Supporting roles in several other movies followed, including *Set It Off* (1996), *Living Out Loud* (1998), and *Chicago* (2002), for which she received an Oscar nomination for Best Supporting Actress.

The versatile performer is also a spokesperson for CoverGirl cosmetics, Curvation ladies underwear, Pizza Hut, and Jenny Craig. She also has a perfume line called Queen.

Queen Latifa (L) costarred with Jennifer Hudson in **The Secret Life of Bees.**

costarred Queen Latifah, Alicia Keys, and Dakota Fanning. The movie about the lives of a group of black women and one white child in the South during the 1960s was adapted from the novel of the same name by Sue Monk Kidd. Hudson played the character of Rosaleen, who is beaten and arrested while trying to vote in a South Carolina town. Like *Sex and the City*, *The Secret Life of Bees* received mixed reviews. A.O. Scott of the *New York Times* said it was "a familiar and tired fable."[44] Roger Ebert found it an unrealistic and inaccurate portrayal of life in the South during the civil rights era, but called it "enchanting"[45] nonetheless. The movie review website Rotten Tomatoes echoed Ebert's sentiments with its report: "The Secret Life of Bees has moments of charm, but is largely too maudlin and sticky-sweet."[46] Although reviewers did not single out Hudson, she did receive a nomination for an NAACP Award for Outstanding Supporting Actress in a Motion Picture for her performance in the movie.

One of the biggest honors Hudson received during this time came on August 28, 2008, at the Democratic National Convention in Denver. She was invited by a fellow Chicagoan, Illinois senator Barack Obama, who at the time was campaigning for the presidency, to sing the national anthem on the last day of the convention. Her stirring performance of "The Star-Spangled Banner" at Invesco Field was broadcast live on national television.

A Whirlwind Romance

Hudson had experienced incredible changes in her professional life in just a few short years. During this time, major changes occurred in her personal life, as well. She and James Payton had been dating for seven years when Hudson won the Oscar. Now that she was a big star, many wondered whether the romance would last. Barbara Walters suggested as much when she interviewed Hudson on Walters's traditional post–Oscar night show: "Jennifer, realistically, James is a maintenance engineer in Chicago. Now you've got Hollywood, you're going to London, you're going to Paris, there's stuff, there's things. It changes relationships sometimes, doesn't it?"[47] Hudson replied to Walters's observation, "We are happy with the place we are right now, but perhaps we will tie the knot someday."[48] In late 2007, however, the couple decided to go their separate ways.

The following spring, Hudson met David Otunga, a graduate of the University of Illinois and of Harvard Law School. Otunga was also a reality TV actor. He had appeared as a contestant nicknamed Punk on the VH1 show *I Love New York 2*, a reality dating show in which twenty men compete for the honor of getting to date the show's star, Tiffany Pollard. Otunga had been eliminated from the show in episode ten of the first season, in December 2007. Otunga and Hudson met in May 2008 and soon began dating. He accompanied her to several promotional events for her movies and upcoming album, and he was in the audience, alongside Hudson's mother, for her performance at the Democratic National Convention.

Seven months after the couple met, Otunga planned a surprise for Hudson. He took her to a beach near Los Angeles on her twenty-seventh birthday, September 12, 2008. There, he had a picnic laid out for her. Later, he handed her a plastic shovel and told her a present was buried in the sand. As she dug, she found card after card from him declaring his love for her. When she turned to face him, he dropped down on one knee and asked her to marry him. Hudson tearfully said yes, though the couple did not set a wedding date at that time.

Everything seemed to be going Hudson's way in the fall of 2008. With a diamond-and-platinum engagement ring on her finger, a recently released album, and her latest movie, *The Secret Life of Bees,* opening in October of that year, her career and personal life were going strong. However, within a few short days of the release of her latest film, an unthinkable tragedy threatened to derail everything for Hudson.

Chapter 5

A Dreamgirl's Nightmare

On the morning of Friday, October 24, 2008, Jennifer Hudson awoke happy. Her latest film, *The Secret Life of Bees,* had opened only a week before and was playing in theaters across the nation, including in her hometown of Chicago. Less than a month before, her debut album had been released, and it had already sold nearly half a million copies. Hudson was looking forward to spending some time celebrating her success with her new fiancé. That weekend, they planned to fly from the home they shared in Florida to Los Angeles, where she and her costars were scheduled to appear on Monday to receive an award honoring the ensemble cast of *The Secret Life of Bees.* But these plans were soon canceled when Hudson received horrific news that changed her life forever.

A Chilling Discovery

At 3:00 on the afternoon of October 24, Jennifer's sister, Julia Hudson, returned from work to the family home on South Yale Avenue in Chicago's South Side. When she opened the door, she was met by a grisly sight. The body of her mother, Darnell, lay in a pool of blood on the living room floor. She had been shot to death. Julia immediately called the authorities. When the police arrived, they discovered the body of Jason Hudson, Jennifer and Julia's brother, in a bedroom. He, too, had been shot to death.

Julia's seven-year-old son, Julian King, had been home from school that day because of teacher meetings. Police searched the entire house, but there was no sign of the second-grader. There was also no sign of forced entry. Investigators believed the shooter had fired through a door and struck Jason first, then entered the house and continued to shoot, hitting Jason's mother when she ran into the living room. The slayings were believed to have occurred between 8:00 and 9:00 that morning. Neighbors had heard shots ring out, but gunfire was so common in the neighborhood that no one had bothered to call 911. This allowed the killer a six- to seven-hour head start before the discovery of the bodies.

Friends and neighbors placed flowers and gifts outside the Hudson family home where Jennifer Hudson's mother and brother were found murdered.

The authorities issued an AMBER Alert (a child abduction alert) for Julian King early that evening. Included in the alert was the boy's stepfather, twenty-seven-year-old William Balfour, who was also missing and was considered a suspect. Balfour, Julia's estranged husband, was an ex-con who had served nearly seven years in prison for carjacking and attempted murder. He had missed a meeting with his parole officer early in the afternoon on the day of the slayings. The parole officer reached Balfour on his cell phone, and Balfour told the officer he was babysitting on the West Side. The parole officer later reported that he heard a child's voice in the background.

Shortly after the AMBER Alert was issued, police tracked Balfour through his cell phone records to his girlfriend's apartment on the West Side. Balfour was arrested, but Julian was not with him. There was also no sign of Jason Hudson's white SUV, which was missing from the Hudsons' home. The police suspected that Balfour had taken Julian away from the home in the car.

Holding Out Hope

Jennifer Hudson immediately flew to Chicago from Florida when she learned what had happened. She was given the difficult task of identifying the bodies of her mother and brother at the morgue late that night, at 1:30 A.M. The double murder was horrifying, but Jennifer and the rest of the family held out hope that little Julian was still alive. In the morning, the FBI was called in to search for the missing child, since authorities believed he may

Murder Capital of the Nation

The Englewood neighborhood, located on the southwest side of Chicago, was a particularly rough place when Jennifer Hudson was growing up, and the crime rate remains high today. In fact, the approximately forty thousand residents of the neighborhood had become so used to the sound of gunfire that on the morning of October 24, 2008, no one even bothered to call the police when shots rang out in the Hudson home. That weekend, as friends, family, and officials combed the area looking for the missing Julian King, at first the presence of so many watchful eyes caused the crime rate to drop and the streets to remain calm. However, by that Sunday, a woman was murdered in Chicago, bringing the homicide total for the city to over 430 so far that year. That is more homicides than occurred in both New York City, with 417, and Los Angeles, with 302, up to that point in 2008, prompting some to call Chicago the nation's murder capital. Despite the city's rampant crime, and especially in the Englewood neighborhood, Darnell Hudson refused to move away from her beloved family home, even after her daughter became famous and successful.

Crime is rampant in the South Side Chicago neighborhood that Jennifer Hudson and her family called home.

have been taken out of state. Detectives worked around the clock. Dozens of officers joined family and friends in searching for the boy or for information as to his whereabouts.

On Saturday, the day after the murders, police searched the Hudson home more thoroughly, in case Julian was hiding somewhere in the house. There was still no sign of him, but police did recover shell casings. That evening, with Julian missing for nearly thirty-six hours, Jennifer and her family made a public plea, offering a $100,000 reward for his safe return. Jennifer also posted this message on her MySpace page: "Thank you all for your prayers and your calls. Please keep praying for our family and that we get Julian King back home safely."[49]

Friends and neighbors gave tremendous support to the grieving, frantic family, helping to comb the area in search of the boy. Angela Russell, a next-door neighbor of the Hudsons, told an interviewer for *The Early Show* on CBS, "There's no words of comfort that anybody can offer at this point. I think the only thing the family really feels will comfort them is having Julian in their arms, knowing that he is safe and okay."[50]

Everyone clung to hopes that Julian would be found alive. Then, early in the morning of Monday, October 27, Chicago resident John Louden, who lived only a couple of miles from Balfour's girlfriend, made a chilling discovery outside his home. A white SUV had been parked near Louden's house since noon on Friday. On Monday morning, Louden's dog ran up to the car and began to bark and howl in a way the man had never before heard. Unsettled by his pet's reaction, Louden wrote down the license number and returned to his house. His wife had written down the license number of the missing Hudson vehicle that was issued in the AMBER Alert bulletins about Julian's disappearance. When they compared the numbers and realized that the SUV was the one police were looking for, Louden called the authorities. Police arrived within two minutes.

They found the worst scene imaginable. The body of Julian King was inside the car, clothed in a T-shirt and basketball shorts. He was slumped over in the backseat. He had been shot once in the head and was pronounced dead at the scene. A gun was also found near the car, and police determined that the gun had been used to kill all three victims.

Once again, it fell to Jennifer to identify her loved one at the morgue. She remained calm when she saw Julian's body, saying only, "Yes, that is him."[51]

The Primary Suspect

Police investigators continued to search for clues in the triple homicide. The primary suspect was William Balfour, who had moved out of the Hudson family home in May 2008 when he and Julia Hudson separated. At the time of the murders, Balfour was still on parole for the 1999 carjacking and attempted murder conviction.

Now in custody, Balfour denied any involvement in the murders. After two days of questioning, he stopped cooperating with police in the investigation and was returned to state prison for violating his parole. At this point, he still had not been charged in connection with the slayings. But he could be kept in state custody until his parole hearing, which could take weeks to occur. In this way, authorities could keep a close eye on him while the homicide investigation continued.

Eventually, police gathered enough evidence for prosecutors to charge Balfour on December 2, 2008, with three counts of first-degree murder. A day later, a judge ordered him held without bail. Balfour continued to deny any involvement in the murders and pleaded not guilty at a hearing the following month. In August 2010, he was granted a continuance, a postponement of the trial to allow his attorneys more time to prepare a defense. The case had yet to go to trial as of early 2011.

Searching for a Motive

Jamie Foxx, who had appeared in *Dreamgirls* opposite Hudson, summed up the reaction of people all across America to the murders when he said, "It was something so evil and foul. How could somebody be that evil to somebody so nice?"[52]

Julia Hudson (L), Jennifer Hudson's sister, stands with Greg King (R), the father of her seven-year-old son Julian, as they plead for Julian's safe return during a press conference after returning home to find her mother, 57-year-old Darnell Hudson Donerson, and her brother, Jason, shot to death and her son missing.

Investigators in the case believed they had unraveled the reasons behind Balfour's alleged violence. Balfour and Julia Hudson had had several heated arguments in the time period leading up to the murders. One of these arguments concerned Balfour's jealous suspicions that his estranged wife was dating someone new. In addition, he had threatened to take Julian away from her. He even threatened her family, according to prosecutors, who said during a hearing that Balfour told his wife "her family would suffer if he saw her with other men."[53]

Another argument, which took place on the morning of the murders, was over car payments. Julia was told that morning by her employers at the bus company where she worked as a driver that her wages would be garnished (a portion withheld) in order

Fragments

Jennifer Hudson had a small role in the movie *Fragments* (2009). The movie is based on the novel *Winged Creatures* by Roy Freirich. The story traces the lives of a group of strangers who survive a random shooting in a restaurant. Each one finds his or her own way to cope in the aftermath of the tragedy. The movie deals with post-traumatic stress and has certain parallels to Hudson's real-life experience, a coincidence because it was filmed before the murders of her family members.

Fragments has the additional distinction of featuring three performers who were nominated for an Academy Award in 2006: Jennifer Hudson, Forest Whitaker, and Jackie Earle Haley. Hudson and Whitaker went on to win the Oscar in their respective categories. It also reunited Hudson with Dakota Fanning, with whom she costarred in *The Secret Life of Bees*. Although *Fragments* was filmed in 2008, its release was delayed for several months, in part because of Hudson's family tragedy. The movie had a limited theatrical release and met with a lukewarm response from the critics before it was released on DVD in August 2009.

to make the car payments. She called Balfour to complain, because he was supposed to have been making some of the car payments. After the phone call, Balfour went to the Hudson home. Witnesses reported that he arrived at the home around 7 A.M. He and Julia Hudson continued the argument there before leaving separately. Julia headed off to work, but, prosecutors allege, Balfour returned to the house a short time later with a gun.

No Greater Loss

Condolences for Jennifer Hudson and her remaining family poured in from the public in the days and weeks following the murders. Members of the local community lined the street outside the family home with flowers, candles, and teddy bears. Several of her fellow castmates, including Queen Latifah and Sarah Jessica Parker, spoke out publicly to offer her their thoughts and prayers. The judges from *American Idol* also made statements, calling the slayings appalling and horrific. Paula Abdul commented, "I personally can't imagine a greater loss for any family."[54] Even fellow Chicagoan Barack Obama, the Democratic nominee for the presidency in the last weeks before the election, sent Hudson words of sympathy and support.

Hudson went into seclusion on the day of the murders, emerging once to make a public plea for her nephew's return, then again to identify his body. She mourned in private and did not attend the public memorial held for her slain family members the week following the murders. The memorial for all three family members was attended by approximately twenty-five hundred people, who filed past the open caskets to pay their respects. Mourners included celebrities such as Oprah Winfrey, Queen Latifah, rapper Missy Elliot, and record producer Clive Davis. Jesse Jackson and Chicago mayor Richard Daley spoke during the service, and Fantasia Barrino and George Huff, both finalists during Hudson's season on *American Idol,* each sang at the service.

Although she did not attend the public memorial, she did attend a private service held a few days later. The grief-stricken Hudson managed to maintain her composure at the funeral. "Jennifer is the pillar," family friend Glover Lewis commented. "It's obvious she's holding the family together."[55]

In Seclusion

Hudson remained in seclusion for months afterward as she tried to come to grips with the loss of her mother, brother, and nephew. She said later during an interview that she spent two weeks straight inside one room, with only family and friends coming in and out, avoiding the press and trying to find a way to deal with her pain. She turned town a movie role because, as she explained, "I was pretty much secluded from everything that was going on. I didn't watch any TV, I didn't want to even know what was going on, because I had more than enough to deal with. I remember

After the brutal murders of her mother, brother, and nephew, Jennifer Hudson went into seclusion for many months, neither granting interviews nor giving performances.

being asked to do a film around that same time, and I was like, 'I have to get adjusted to who I am now, so I can't be another character if I don't know who I am.'"[56]

In addition to turning down scripts in the aftermath of the tragedy, Hudson also postponed the release of the second single from her album *Jennifer Hudson*. "My Heart" was originally scheduled to be released in late October 2008, but after the slayings she rescheduled the song's release for the following January. In the meantime, the record company decided the second release would instead be "If This Isn't Love," which eventually came out in February 2009.

During the time Hudson remained in seclusion, she did not speak out publicly about the murders. She would later recall her mourning period as a big blur. "It was surreal. It was like I was outside of myself," she later explained. Hudson relied on her faith to stay strong during this time, and says she turned to prayer to help herself cope. "I would pray when I get up in the morning and pray before I lay down at night."[57] She also comforted herself with her belief that her family members had gone on to a better place.

Chapter 6

Life Goes On

After more than three months in seclusion, Jennifer Hudson finally took the first brave steps back to public life. When she returned, true to her resilient nature, she did it in a big way, with a flurry of public performances beginning in February 2009. She kicked off her triumphant comeback with an appearance on national television before 98.7 million viewers: Super Bowl XLIII, the most-watched Super Bowl in history.

"She's on Fire Right Now"

On February 1, 2009, Hudson sang "The Star-Spangled Banner" at the Super Bowl, held in Tampa, Florida, and televised on NBC. Hudson looked a little nervous when she took the stage, but she took a deep breath and began to sing. Like most performers at the Super Bowl, Hudson lip-synched, at the request of the game's musical producer; there are too many things that can go wrong to permit a live performance. Despite the lip-synching, it was a very touching rendition, and those in attendance in the stadium—including some of the football players—were clearly moved. After her performance, when she returned to her dressing room, she found a text message on her cell phone from *Dreamgirls* costar Jamie Foxx, in which he told her she had brought tears to his eyes.

American Idol music director Ricky Minor, who has served as

After three months out of the public eye, Jennifer Hudson reappeared to sing the national anthem for the Super Bowl MXLIII pregame show.

the pregame show producer for numerous Super Bowl games, was the producer for Super Bowl XLIII. After Hudson's performance, Minor told the Associated Press that Hudson was in great spirits that day. Then he summed up: "She's on fire right now and totally grounded."[58]

Indeed, Hudson threw herself into a whirlwind of public performances after the Super Bowl. She performed at the 51st Grammy Awards ceremony on February 8, 2009, and on the same occasion received a Grammy for her debut album. This special moment for Hudson was made even more special because the award was presented to her by one of her idols, Whitney Houston, who called Hudson "absolutely one of the greatest voices of our time."[59] Hudson gave a very emotional acceptance speech. When she sang "You Pulled Me Through" from her album, she teared up toward the end. The song took on special meaning in light of what had happened to her family. Ricky Minor said her performance "just reaches straight through the television, just grabs your heart. . . . It was just amazing."[60]

Hudson next appeared at the 40th NAACP Image Awards ceremony, broadcast live from the Shrine Auditorium in Los Angeles on February 12, 2009. She won three awards, including the award for Outstanding New Artist. On this occasion, she gave an emotional performance of the song "The Impossible Dream" as a tribute to boxing legend Muhammad Ali. She also appeared as a guest on season 8 of *American Idol* the following April, and she gave a live performance of "If This Isn't Love," the second single from her album.

Throwing Herself into Performing

Having successfully stepped back into the spotlight, Hudson threw herself into her music. She gave numerous other public performances as 2009 progressed, including an appearance in an all-star tribute to Neil Diamond in which she sang his 1969 hit "Holly Holy." Hudson received a standing ovation for her performance, and rap-rocker Kid Rock, who performed next, joked backstage afterward, "I'm gonna kill whoever made me follow

Jennifer Hudson. Thanks!"[61]

She continued making public appearances that summer and fall, notably at the memorial service for Michael Jackson shortly after his death, singing Jackson's "Will You Be There." (Hudson later performed in the star-studded tribute to Michael Jackson on the 2010 Grammy Awards show.) In September 2009 she performed "Spotlight" for the *VH1 Divas* concert, which also included Paula Abdul, Sheryl Crow, Cyndi Lauper, Melissa Etheridge, Martina McBride, Leona Lewis, Kelly Clarkson, and Miley Cyrus, among others.

In September 2010 Hudson performed in a concert that was very close to her heart. She celebrated her twenty-ninth birthday by performing in a gospel concert at Christ Universal Temple in Chicago. All proceeds from the concert went to the Julian King Foundation, set up in honor of her late nephew, to provide gifts for children during the holiday season.

Jennifer Pours Her Heart Out

Although Hudson has released only one album so far, she has made numerous contributions to various other works, including the recording of "We Are the World: 25 for Haiti." This charity single was a remake of 1985's blockbuster single "We Are the World," cowritten by Michael Jackson to raise money to fight famine in Africa. The remake, which features more than eighty artists, was produced to help provide relief following the devastating earthquake in Haiti in January 2010. Hudson also performed the Beatles anthem "Let It Be" for the Hope for Haiti Now telethon to raise funds for people left homeless after the earthquake. And, although her character did not appear in the sequel to *Sex and the City*, Hudson sang a duet with Leona Lewis, "Love Is Your Color," on the soundtrack for *Sex and the City 2* (2010).

Hudson has also collaborated with and appeared on recordings for other artists. She recorded the song "The Future Ain't What It Used to Be" with the singer Meat Loaf on his 2006 album, *Bat out of Hell III: The Monster Is Loose*. She sang "Leaving Tonight" as a guest vocalist on rhythm-and-blues and pop singer-song-

Jennifer Hudson performs at the 'We Are The World: 25 Years for Haiti' recording session

writer Ne-Yo's 2007 album, *Because of You*. She contributed "The Star-Spangled Banner" to the compilation album *Change Is Now: Renewing America's Promise,* released in 2009 in conjunction with the Presidential Inaugural Committee. And in 2010, she contributed to a compilation album by music legend Quincy Jones, who had served as producer and conductor of the original recording of "We Are the World" as well as producer of the song's remake. Jones told an interviewer for *Rolling Stone* magazine that when he called Hudson after the loss of her family, she begged him to let her sing on his new album, which was to feature various artists.

He at first did not want to bother her in her time of grief, but she insisted, telling him, "Quincy, you don't understand—I need to be on that album."[62] Hudson contributed "You Put a Move on My Heart" to his *Q: Soul Bossa Nostra*, released in November 2010.

"The Light of My Day"

These days, Jennifer Hudson's personal life is also keeping her very busy. On August 10, 2009, the twenty-seven-year-old Hudson

A Friend of the President

Jennifer Hudson is one of the many people who count President Barack Obama among their friends. Hudson has performed at many events at the invitation of Obama, beginning with her rendition of the national anthem at the Democratic National Convention in August 2008. Obama invited her to appear with him at a fund-raiser for the Democratic National Committee in Beverly Hills in May 2009, and she headlined the concert that night. More recently, Hudson sang at an event hosted on February 9, 2010, by the president and First Lady Michelle Obama. Called "In Performance at the White House: A Celebration of Music from the Civil Rights Movement," the concert held in the East Room of the White House celebrated Black History Month and featured music that portrayed struggles of the civil rights era. The event was emceed by Morgan Freeman and Queen Latifah and featured performances by several artists in addition to Hudson, including Natalie Cole, Bob Dylan, John Legend, John Mellencamp, Smokey Robinson, Seal, the Blind Boys of Alabama, and the Howard University Choir.

Jennifer Hudson performs at the 2008 Democratic National Convention in Denver, where then-Senator Barack Obama accepted the Democratic nomination to become the first African American candidate for president.

and her fiancé, David Otunga, welcomed their son, David Daniel Otunga Jr., into the world. Hudson adores being a mother and has called her new baby "the light of my day."[63] She also finds comfort in the new life she was able to bring into the world after losing three of her family members and says, "Being a mother reminds me of my mom." She adds, "I want him to get the same love and the same upbringing as my mother gave us, and I know for sure that way he'll be loved."[64]

She says that little David loves her three Pomeranian dogs, which she named Dreamgirl, Oscar, and Grammy. Because he has played with them all of his young life, Hudson says he thinks he is one of them and growls like a dog at objects and even people. Hudson finds it funny that her young son thinks humans communicate by growling, just like dogs.

Apart from playing with the dogs, one of her son's favorite things is music. When he was an infant, he would calm down immediately whenever his mother would sing or play the piano. And, much as his mother hit a high note in church one day as a baby, little David has already shown an interest in singing. Otunga explains that when David was only a few months old, he began to imitate the notes he was hearing as a man tuned the piano in their home in Tampa, Florida. Declared Otunga, "It was the most amazing thing."[65]

Hudson and Otunga are also busy planning their wedding. They announced in March 2010 that they had set a wedding date. They did not make the date public, but did say they planned to hold the wedding in Chicago.

A Healthier, Slimmer Jennifer

As thrilled as she is to be a mother, there was one result of her pregnancy that did not make Hudson happy: her weight gain. Hudson has struggled to control her weight for years. She first felt pressure to lose weight when she was performing for talent competitions and for nightclubs back in Chicago. She resisted the pressure, however, in part because she was comfortable with her voluptuous figure, but also because she was afraid her voice would not sound the same if she were thin. She told an interviewer in 2006, "I have a little singer's pouch, and that's where the voice comes from, so you're all just going to have to get used to my jelly."[66] She endured much criticism in the tabloids and in blogs, however, after the release of her album, because her picture on the cover appeared to have been digitally altered to make her look thinner. Hudson refused to comment publicly on either the cover or the criticism of it.

Hudson had deliberately packed on an additional 20 pounds (9kg) to play the role of Effie White in *Dreamgirls*. The movie's director asked her to keep the weight on for several months after filming ended, so that she would still be heavy for the promotional events for the film. She eventually lost the weight she had

After a year on the Weight Watchers program, Jennifer lost eighty pounds. Here she teams up with Weight Watchers for the "Lose for Good" campaign, to fight hunger and obesity.

gained for the movie, but then regained it—and more—during her pregnancy. After having spent years dieting and watching her weight go up and down, Hudson decided after the birth of her son to join Weight Watchers. After losing her first 50 pounds (22.7kg), Hudson became a spokesperson for Weight Watchers in April 2010. She appears on the company's website and in TV commercials to promote the company—and a healthy lifestyle.

By October 2010, after one year of following the Weight Watchers diet and an intense workout schedule, she had lost 80 pounds (36.3kg) and ten dress sizes. She said she felt good about her new, healthier body. Her primary motivation for the weight loss, however, remains her fiancé and her new baby. "I want to be a good role model to my son,"[67] Hudson told *OK!* magazine in October 2010.

What's Next?

Hudson spent the summer of 2010 in South Africa, filming the movie *Winnie*. She stars in the role of Winnie Mandela, the controversial politician and ex-wife of South Africa's elder statesman Nelson Mandela, who served as the country's president from 1994 to 1999. The movie finished shooting in September 2010 and is scheduled for release in 2011.

After wrapping up her work on *Winnie*, Hudson returned to the recording studio and began to work on a second album. Titled *I Remember Me,* released March 22, 2011, via Arista Records. Hudson says she wanted this album to be "more personal than the first album, and just more me,"[68] indicating that she planned to be more involved in the process of making the album than she was for her first album.

Hudson has also indicated her desire to act in more movies, including serious dramas. She told an interviewer for *Empress* magazine that one story she would be interested in working on would be that of Jackie Robinson, the first African American major league baseball player. Hudson explained, "It is something that's interesting and special and of course it is about our culture and history. I like to do things with substance and a meaning."[69]

Winnie Mandela

Winnie Mandela is a South African political activist. She is known for advocating violent resistance to apartheid, a form of segregation that was legal in South Africa until 1991. Born Nomzamo Winifred Zanyiwe Madikizela in 1936, she married Nelson Mandela, a leader in the African National Congress (ANC) opposition, in 1958. When her husband was imprisoned in 1963, she continued his antiapartheid activism with the ANC during his twenty-seven-year confinement. For her activities with the ANC, she was exiled and confined to the township of Brandfort in central South Africa. In 1969 she was arrested and spent eighteen months in solitary confinement.

Although the Nobel Peace Prize–winning Nelson Mandela is widely admired, Winnie remains a controversial figure. She and Nelson divorced in 1996 amid allegations of corruption, illegal activity, and infidelity during his long incarceration. People have differing views of her: Her supporters refer to her as "Mother of the Nation," yet many others see her as a ruthless criminal. The most notable example of this is the 1989 kidnapping and murder of a fourteen-year-old boy by members of her security staff. She was convicted of kidnapping and being an accessory to assault and given a six-year jail sentence, which was later reduced to a fine. In 2003 she was convicted of forty-three counts of fraud, for which she never served any prison time.

She also says that she would love to appear in a comedy, because it would challenge her in ways she has not been challenged yet. But above all, she says she wants to continue to do both acting and singing.

Hudson says she would also like to have one more baby—this time, a girl. She says, however, that she wants to wait a few years before having another child. However many children she winds up having, one thing is for sure: Her children can be proud to call Jennifer Hudson their mother, because she has an inner strength and a sense of determination and perseverance that she can pass on to her kids. After her elimination from *American Idol,* Hudson expressed some thoughts about her experience on the show that could just as easily be applied to her life today and beyond: "It's been a struggle, it hasn't been easy, but if it's not worth working hard for, it's not worth it at all. So, I'm proud of the struggle that I've been going through, and I'm making it. I'm a survivor."[70]

Introduction: A Chicago Girl

1. Jennifer Hudson, interview by David Letterman. *The Late Show with David Letterman.* CBS, January 8, 2007.
2. Quoted in Dave Hoekstra. "Living the Dream: Jennifer Hudson Brings Truth, Clarity to 'Dreamgirls' Role." *Chicago Sun-Times,* December 16, 2006. www.suntimes.com /entertainment/175911,sho-cst-dream17.article.
3. Quoted in *Access Hollywood.* "Jennifer Hudson: The Girl Behind the 'Dream.'" December 17, 2006. http://today.msnbc.msn .com/id/16258193/ns/today-entertainment.
4. Quoted in *Jennifer Hudson: I'll Be Home for Christmas,* Holiday special. ABC, December 14, 2009.

Chapter 1: Humble Beginnings

5. Quoted in Nick Curtis. "Oscar Hope Hudson Brings Down the House." *London Evening Standard*, January 25, 2007. www .thisislondon.co.uk/film/article-23383042-oscar-hope-hudson-brings-down-the-house.do.
6. Quoted in *Behind the Music.* "Jennifer Hudson." Episode 213, VH1, June 28, 2010.
7. Quoted in Robert K. Elder. "Though Hudson's Career Took Off, Her Family Here Kept Her Grounded." *Chicago Tribune,* October 26, 2008. http://articles.chicagotribune.com/2008-10-26/news/0810250298_1_jennifer-hudson-hip-hop-albums-mother.
8. Quoted in *Behind the Music.* "Jennifer Hudson."
9. Quoted in Curtis. "Oscar Hope Hudson Brings Down the House."
10. Quoted in Hoekstra. "Living the Dream."
11. Quoted in *Behind the Music.* "Jennifer Hudson."
12. Quoted in *Jennifer Hudson: I'll Be Home for Christmas.*
13. Quoted in Hoekstra. "Living the Dream."
14. Quoted in Hoekstra. "Living the Dream."

Chapter 2: Following Her Heart

15. Quoted in Hoekstra. "Living the Dream."
16. Quoted in Hoekstra. "Living the Dream."
17. Quoted in *Empress*. "Jennifer Hudson—Something Like a Dream." www.empressmag.com/interviews/jennifer-hudson-something-like-a-dream.
18. Quoted in Lisa Frydman. "Jennifer Hudson, No Longer at Bay." *Chicago Sun-Times,* August 1, 2004.
19. Quoted in *People*. "Jennifer Hudson." www.people.com/people/jennifer_hudson/biography/0,20159710,00.html.

Chapter 3: Stepping into the Spotlight on *American Idol*

20. Quoted in *American Idol*, season 3, episode 2. Fox Broadcasting Company, January 20, 2004.
21. Quoted in *American Idol*, season 3, episode 9. Fox Broadcasting Company, February 10, 2004.
22. Quoted in *Barbara Walters Oscar Special*. ABC, February 25, 2007.
23. Quoted in *American Idol,* season 3, episode 9.
24. Quoted in *American Idol,* season 3, episode 9.
25. Quoted in *American Idol,* season 3, episode 18. Fox Broadcasting Company, March 9, 2004.
26. Quoted in *American Idol,* season 3, episode 18.
27. Quoted in Sean Smith. "Living the Dream." *Newsweek*, December 11, 2006. www.newsweek.com/2006/12/03/living-the-dream.html.
28. Lola Ogunnaike. "And the Mirror Says: Go for It, Dreamgirl." *New York Times*, February 27, 2007.
29. Quoted in *American Idol,* season 3, episode 30. Fox Broadcasting Company, April 21, 2004.
30. Quoted in *American Idol,* season 3, episode 30.
31. Quoted in *American Idol,* season 3, episode 30.
32. Quoted in A. Simigis. "Reality Might: 'American Idol' Champ Fantasia Barrino Storms the Charts." *Chicago Tribune*, August 4, 2004. www.chicagotribune.com/search/mmx-040804-musicfantasia,0,7764336.story.
33. Quoted in Associated Press. "Elton John Says 'American Idol' Vote Is 'Racist.'" *USA Today,* April 28, 2004. www.usatoday.com/life/people/2004-04-28-elton-john-idol_x.htm.

34. Quoted in *Behind the Music*. "Jennifer Hudson."
35. Quoted in American Idol.com. "Jennifer Hudson." www .americanidol.com/archive/contestants/season3/jennifer_ hudson.

Chapter 4: Dreams Come True

36. Roger Ebert. "Ebert's Oscar Predictions." *Chicago Sun-Times*, February 10, 2007. http://rogerebert.suntimes.com/apps/pbcs .dll/article?AID=/20070210/OSCARS/70210001.
37. Peter Travers. "Dreamgirls." *Rolling Stone*, November 21, 2006. www.rollingstone.com/movies/reviews/dreamgirls-20061121.
38. Quoted in Hudson. interview by David Letterman.
39. Quoted in Curtis. "Oscar Hope Hudson Brings Down the House."
40. Jennifer Hudson acceptance speech. *79th Academy Awards*. ABC, February 25, 2007.
41. Manohla Dargis. "The Girls Are Back in Town." *New York Times*, May 30, 2008. http://movies.nytimes.com/2008/05/30 /movies/30sex.html.
42. Ramin Setoodeh. "Sexism and the City." *Newsweek*, June 3, 2008. www.newsweek.com/2008/06/02/sexism-and-the-city.html.
43. Carina Chocano. "Review: 'Sex and the City.'" *Los Angeles Times*, May 30, 2008. www.latimes.com/entertainment/news/reviews /movies/la-et-sex30-2008may30,0,6188162.story.
44. A. O. Scott. "A Golden Dollop of Motherly Comfort." *New York Times*, October 17, 2008. http://movies.nytimes .com/2008/10/17/movies/17bees.html.
45. Roger Ebert. "The Secret Life of Bees." *Chicago Sun-Times*, October 15, 2008. http://rogerebert.suntimes.com/apps/pbcs .dll/article?AID=/20081015/REVIEWS/810150281.
46. Rotten Tomatoes. "The Secret Life of Bees (2008)." www .rottentomatoes.com/m/secret_life_of_bees.
47. Quoted in *Barbara Walters Oscar Special*.
48. Quoted in *Barbara Walters Oscar Special*.

Chapter 5: From Dreams to Nightmares

49. Quoted in CBS News. October 27, 2008.
50. Quoted in *The Early Show*. CBS News, October 27, 2008.

51. Quoted in Annie Sweeney et al. "Julia Hudson, Husband Argued Over Car Payments Morning of Murders: Sources." *Chicago Sun-Times,* October 28, 2008. www.suntimes.com/news/24-7/1245829,jennifer-hudson-murders-possible-motive-102808.article.

52. Quoted in *Behind the Music.* "Jennifer Hudson."

53. Quoted in Daniel Kreps. "Jennifer Hudson's Family Killed In 'Jealous Rage,' Say Prosecutors." *Rolling Stone,* December 4, 2008. www.rollingstone.com/music/news/14844/92418.

54. Quoted in Daniel Kreps. "Cowell, Abdul Send Condolences to Jennifer Hudson." *Rolling Stone,* October 28, 2008. www.rollingstone.com/music/news/14844/86691.

55. Quoted in Stacy St. Clair and Azam Ahmed. "'Idol' Lift for Hudson at Emotional Funeral." *Chicago Breaking News Center,* November 3, 2008. www.chicagobreakingnews.com/2008/11/services-held-for-slain-hudson-family-members.html.

56. Quoted in *Behind the Music.* "Jennifer Hudson."

57. Quoted in *Behind the Music.* "Jennifer Hudson."

Chapter 6: Life Goes On

58. Quoted in Associated Press. "Hudson Shines in Singing National Anthem at Super Bowl." February 1, 2009. www.nfl.com/superbowl/story?id=09000d5d80e818f7&template=with-video-with-comments&confirm=true.

59. Quoted in *Behind the Music.* "Jennifer Hudson."

60. Quoted in *Behind the Music.* "Jennifer Hudson."

61. Quoted in *Rolling Stone.* "Dave Grohl, Coldplay, Jennifer Hudson Lead All-Star Tribute to Neil Diamond at MusiCares Gala." February 7, 2009. www.rollingstone.com/music/news/15765/92190.

62. Quoted in Andy Greene. "Quincy Jones on Recording with Amy Winehouse and His Rough Chicago Upbringing." *Rolling Stone,* September 7, 2010. www.rollingstone.com/music/news/17386/210810.

63. Quoted in Luis Arroyave. "Jennifer Hudson Discusses Her Upcoming Chicago Wedding and Her Fiance's Wrestling Career." *Chicago Tribune,* March 31, 2010. http://leisureblogs.chicagotribune.com/about-last-night/2010/03/jennifer-hudson-on-her-upcoming-wedding-in-chicago.html.

64. Quoted in *Behind the Music*. "Jennifer Hudson."
65. Quoted in Marc Malkin. "Jennifer Hudson's Baby Son: A Singing Wrestler?!" E! Online, February 23, 2010. www.eonline.com /uberblog/b168493_jennifer_hudsons_baby_son_singing. html.
66. Quoted in Hoekstra. "Living the Dream."
67. Quoted in *OK!* "Jennifer Hudson on Weight Loss—'I Want to Be a Good Role Model to My Son.'" October 25, 2010. www.okmagazine .com/2010/10/jennifer-hudson-on-weight-loss-%e2%80%94- i-want-to-be-a-good-role-model-to-my-son.
68. Quoted in Phil Wahba. "'Dreamgirls' Star Jennifer Hudson Said on Wednesday She Can't Wait to Perform Again, Now That She Has a Slim New Look." Reuters, September 16, 2010. www.reuters.com /article/idUSTRE68E6EO20100916.
69. Quoted in *Empress*. "Jennifer Hudson—Something Like a Dream."
70. Quoted in *American Idol*. season 3, episode 30.

1981

Jennifer Kate Hudson is born September 12 in Chicago, Illinois.

1998

Jennifer's beloved grandmother, Julia Kate Hudson, dies.

1999

Graduates from high school; begins dating James Payton, a relationship that will last for eight years; briefly attends Langston University before transferring to Kennedy-King College; stepfather, Samuel Simpson, dies.

2001

Cast in Chicago's Marriott Lincolnshire Theatre's production of the musical *Big River*, in which she performs for nearly two years; drops out of college to devote herself to her singing career; sister gives birth to Jennifer's nephew, Julian King.

2003

Performs the role of Calliope in *Hercules: The Musical,* a Disney cruise ship production; turns down second contract with Disney to audition for *American Idol.*

2004

Appears on season 3 of *American Idol,* makes it to the finals, and is eliminated in seventh place; subsequently tours the United States with the American Idol Live! tour; appears on Broadway in one-night Actors Fund of America benefit performance of the rock musical *Hair*.

2006

Appears in *Dreamgirls* and goes on to win the Academy Award for Best Supporting Actress for her performance as Effie White.

2007

Becomes a spokesperson for Avon's Imari fragrance line; becomes the first African American singer and only the third African American celebrity to appear on the cover of *Vogue* magazine.

2008

Appears in the movies *Sex and the City* and *The Secret Life of Bees*; releases album *Jennifer Hudson*; becomes engaged to David Otunga; her mother, brother, and nephew are murdered in Chicago.

2009

Performs at Super Bowl XLIII; appears in *Fragments*; wins Grammy Award for best rhythm and blues album; gives birth to her first child, David Daniel Otunga Jr.

2010

Performs during the Hope for Haiti Now telethon and sings on the "We Are the World: 25 for Haiti" single to raise funds for Haitian earthquake victims; becomes spokesperson for Weight Watchers; begins work on a second album.

2011

Plays controversial South African politician Winnie Mandela in biopic *Winnie*; releases second album, *I Remember Me*.

For More Information

Books

Sue Monk Kidd. *The Secret Life of Bees.* New York: Penguin, 2002. This novel about family secrets and life in the South in the early 1960s was adapted into a movie starring Queen Latifah, Alicia Keys, Dakota Fanning, and Jennifer Hudson.

Jeanne Nagle. *Jennifer Hudson.* New York: Rosen, 2008. This biography of Hudson describes her rise to national prominence as a singer on reality television.

Gail Snyder. *Jennifer Hudson.* Philadelphia: Mason Crest, 2009. Part of the Dream Big: American Idol Superstars series, this book details Hudson's rise to stardom via the popular reality TV series.

Betsy West. *Jennifer Hudson: American Dream Girl.* New York: Price Stern Sloan, 2007. Explores Hudson's stint on *American Idol* and her success in her debut film, *Dreamgirls.*

Periodicals

Dave Hoekstra. "Living the Dream: Jennifer Hudson Brings Truth, Clarity to 'Dreamgirls' Role." *Chicago Sun-Times,* December 16, 2006.

Daniel Kreps. "Cowell, Abdul Send Condolences to Jennifer Hudson." *Rolling Stone,* October 28, 2008.

Daniel Kreps. "Jennifer Hudson's Family Killed In 'Jealous Rage,' Say Prosecutors." *Rolling Stone,* December 4, 2008.

Tracy Shaffer. "Fun, Fearless Female: Jennifer Hudson." *Cosmopolitan,* June 2008.

Internet Sources

American Idol.com. "Jennifer Hudson." www.americanidol.com/archive/contestants/season3/jennifer_hudson.

Chicago Tribune. "Updated: Timeline in the Murders of Jennifer Hudson Family Members." November 10, 2008. www.chicagotribune.com/chi-jennifer-hudson-murders-timeline,0,2789744.story.

Nick Curtis. "Oscar Hope Hudson Brings Down the House." *London Evening Standard*, January 25, 2007. www.thisislondon.co.uk/film/article-23383042-oscar-hope-hudson-brings-down-the-house.do.

Robert K. Elder. "Though Hudson's Career Took Off, Her Family Here Kept Her Grounded." *Chicago Tribune,* October 26, 2008. http://articles.chicagotribune.com/2008-10-26/news/0810250298_1_jennifer-hudson-hip-hop-albums-mother.

Lee Hildebrand. "Jennifer Hudson Readies New Album, Two Films." *San Francisco Chronicle*, September 7, 2008. http://articles.sfgate.com/2008-09-07/entertainment/17161050_1_jennifer-hudson-dreamgirls-effie-white.

Tim Molloy. "Jennifer Hudson Stays Close to Roots in Tragedy." *TV Guide,* October 27, 2008. www.tvguide.com/News/Jennifer-Hudson-Stays-34760.aspx.

People. "Jennifer Hudson Biography." www.people.com/people/jennifer_hudson/biography.

Stephen M. Silverman. "'Idol' Hopefuls Down to an Even Dozen." *People*, March 11, 2004. www.people.com/people/article/0,,627842,00.html.

Sean Smith. "Living the Dream." *Newsweek*, December 11, 2006. www.newsweek.com/2006/12/03/living-the-dream.html.

Stacy St. Clair and Azam Ahmed. "'Idol' Lift for Hudson at Emotional Funeral." *Chicago Breaking News Center*, November 3, 2008. www.chicagobreakingnews.com/2008/11/services-held-for-slain-hudson-family-members.html.

Annie Sweeney et al. "Julia Hudson, Husband Argued Over Car Payments Morning of Murders: Sources." *Chicago Sun-Times,* October 28, 2008. www.suntimes.com/news/24-7/1245829,jennifer-hudson-murders-possible-motive-102808.article.

Websites

American Idol (www.americanidol.com/archive/contestants/ season3/jennifer_hudson). Jennifer Hudson's page on the *American Idol* website provides basic biographical information on the season 3 contestant.

AOL Music (http://music.aol.com/artist/jennifer-hudson/ albums). Features a list of albums and singles released by Jennifer Hudson as well as lyrics, track lists, reviews, and detailed information on each release.

Dreamgirls Onstage (www.dreamgirlsonstage.com). This is the official site for the national tour of the Broadway production of *Dreamgirls*. The site includes reviews, a photo gallery, videos, song clips, and other information about the film.

Jennifer Hudson (www.jenniferhudson.net). This official fan site for Jennifer Hudson includes a biography, photos, a message board, and more.

Weight Watchers (www.weightwatchers.com/util/art/index_art .aspx?tabnum=1&art_id=84581). Contains a blog maintained by Hudson, video of Hudson discussing her weight loss, a link to her seven-day meal plan, and links to her TV commercials for Weight Watchers, as well as general information about Weight Watchers.

Otunga, David Daniel Jr., 76

P
Payton, James, 23, 24, 55
Personal life
  children, 76, 79
  dating, 23, 24, 55
  engagement, 56
  marriage plans, 76
  weight gain/loss, 76–78
Pleasant Gift Missionary Baptist
  Church, Chicago, 13
Police, 59, 61
Prayer, 67

Q
Queen Latifah, *54*, 55, 65

R
Racism, 43
Recording contracts, 46, 51,
  72–73
Religious influences, 11, 13, 15,
  17
Rolling Stone (magazine), 74
Ross, Diana, *48*, 49
Russell, Angela, 61

S
Scott, A. O., 55
Seacrest, Ryan, 36
Seclusion, 65–67
The Secret Life of Bees (film),
  52–56, 57
Sex and the City (film), 52
Sex and the City 2 (film), 71
Simpson, Samuel (stepfather),
  11, 12, 13, 23

Social functions, 31, 46
Soul Train (musical variety
  show), 18
South Africa, 78, 79
"Star-Spangled Banner" (song),
  55, 68, 74
Studdard, Ruben, 28, *30–31*
Super Bowl, 68, *69*, 70
The Supremes, 47, *48*

T
Talk shows, 44–45, 52
Teenage years
  academic honors, 20, 22
  local productions, 22, 23
  social life, 19–20
"The three divas," 40, 42, 43
Tours, 45
Twain, Mark, 25, 26

V
Vocal range, 32
Vogue (magazine), 52
Voting controversy, 42–44

W
Walters, Barbara, 34, 55
Weight Watchers, 77–78
Wild card rounds, 29, 36, *38*
Williams, Walter, 22
Wilson, Mary, 48
Windham, Debra Nichols (god-
  mother), 13
Winfrey, Oprah, 52, 65
Winnie (film), 78

Cherese Cartlidge holds a bachelor's degree in psychology and a master's degree in education. She currently works as a writer and editor and has written numerous books for children and young adults, including *People in the News: Leonardo DiCaprio*. Cartlidge lives in Georgia with her two children.